From
ROLLO
to
TOM SAWYER
AND OTHER PAPERS

by
Alice M. Jordan

Decorations by Nora S. Unwin

1948
THE HORN BOOK INC., BOSTON

TO

My Mother

*T*hese brief chapters on a few of the nineteenth century writers of books for children make no claim to be more than footnotes to that complete history of American children's books, greatly needed and as yet unwritten.

The paper from which the book takes its title was the first Caroline M. Hewins Lecture, read at Swampscott, Massachusetts, October 18, 1947. Six of the other chapters have appeared at various times in the "Horn Book" which has graciously allowed them to be reprinted with some revision.

Permission to quote from the following is here acknowledged with appreciation: Charles D. Abbott's "Howard Pyle. A Chronicle" (Harper and Brothers); Samuel Crothers' "Miss Muffet's Christmas Party" (Houghton Mifflin Company); Robert Morss Lovett's "Boy's Reading Fifty Years Ago" ("New Republic"); and Howard Pyle's "The Merry Adventures of Robin Hood," Thomas Nelson Page's "Two Little Confederates" and Frances Hodgson Burnett's "The Little Princess" (all Charles Scribner's Sons).

To Harriet Swift, of the Rare Books Department of the Boston Public Library, my cordial thanks are due for her help in securing material on early American publications.

Most of all, I owe a debt of continuing gratitude to Bertha Mahony Miller for her constant sympathy and understanding over the years. Without her unfailing confidence and encouragement "From Rollo to Tom Sawyer and Other Papers" would never have been finished.

A. M. J.

Cambridge
September, 1948

CONTENTS

INTRODUCTORY

I

NY STUDY, like the present, of nineteenth century writers for American children requires at least a brief glance at the book production of earlier years. For while the desirability of juvenile books to meet American needs did not make itself felt before the second quarter of the nineteenth century, there was no lack of activity in behalf of young American readers. A survey of the work of native presses may well be entered upon by reference to the distinguished volume entitled *Early American Children's Books*, describing the famous collection assembled by Dr. A. S. W. Rosenbach, of Philadelphia. In this exhaustive catalogue eight hundred juvenile books, published in the United States between 1682 and 1836, are listed and annotated. The basis of the information contained in the present chapter rests mainly upon an examination of *Early American Children's Books* (Southworth Press).

The nucleus of the collection was the varied stock of Jacob Johnson, a Quaker publisher who did a flourishing business in Philadelphia in the late eighteenth century and continuing into the nineteenth when Moses Polock, then a clerk in the office, acquired it. Although books published in Philadelphia naturally outnumber in the catalogue those from any other one place, it is surprising to learn how extensive the production of children's books really was in the first two hundred years of the English settlement of America.

Nor were the printers and publishers confined to the cities on the seaboard. Before the year 1836 we find that a market had arisen for the publishing output of fifteen states. In New York alone nineteen towns had connections with the publishing business. As a group, New England was in the lead. All her larger communities could show one or more printers who included children's books on their lists. Fourteen towns in Massachusetts and ten in Connecticut made their names known in this way. Isaiah Thomas at Boston and Worcester, Hugh Gaine at New York, John and Sidney Babcock at Hartford and New Haven, William Charles, printer and engraver of Philadelphia—all these are names associated with memorable work. Not a few publishers maintained branch houses. Isaiah Thomas controlled at one time sixteen presses, seven of them in Worcester, as well as bookstores in five states. If such abundance had been attended by a corresponding flow of creative ability, children's literature would have been rich indeed. But we look in vain for titles that have endured to become a part of children's reading today. With a few exceptions of books not written for children they have vanished, save as they are preserved here and there in special libraries.

The period before the Revolution has been called "the dreariest and most sterile in the entire history of American literature." As James Truslow Adams points out, it is the intellectual and aesthetic part of life that suffers in pioneer days.

Until the beginning of the nineteenth century the center for the publication of children's books was in Boston, where the Puritan element took the lead. Shadowed by the "terrible reality of invisible things," life was presented to Puritan children on both sides of the ocean as a hard and cruel bondage from which an early death was to be counted a joyful escape. To understand the depressing popularity of children's books overborne by thoughts of the grave, it is necessary to realize the Puritan's concern with a future life which completely dwarfed all sense of proportion. As we turn the pages of one of the most widely read books of the era, the severity of the prevailing influence makes itself felt in full strength. The book is called *A Token for Children*. It is by James Janeway, a famous English divine whose creed was a harsh and cruel one with no room in it for love and forgiveness. His noted book, printed in England and reprinted many times in America, is devoted to the condemnation of worldly pleasures and to the praise of the life and death of remarkably pious young children. The Boston bookseller, John Usher, imported thirty copies of the *Token* in one shipment.

Perhaps to show that American children were not to be outdone by English ones in piety, Cotton Mather added to the reprinted edition similar life histories of New England infants whose early deaths showed remarkable instances of religious convictions.

If *A Token for Children* and similar books were favorite gifts to the little colonials, John Cotton's *Spiritual Milk for Babes* was a favorite catechism. Like nearly all the others this book was of English origin, but it seems to belong especially to America because its author, the Reverend John Cotton, was the most renowned preacher in both Bostons as well as the most influential Puritan in the whole history of New England. Besides, the Massachusetts reprint bore the name *Spiritual Milk for Boston Babes in Either England.*

From its first appearance his catechism went through many editions and was revived for use in Sunday schools little more than a hundred years ago. It also became a part of a far more important book, *The New-England Primer.* The roots of this famous little book go far back to the Latin "Book of Hours," later called "The Prymer." There were many primers written in Latin, or in English and Latin, varying in form in the different dioceses, called "The Prymer after the use of Salisbury," or of York or Bangor, etc., according to the diocese in which it was prepared and used. Such a primer has been termed the "Lay Folks Prayer

Book," being really a primary—hence primer—manual of church service. The inclusion of the alphabet in many primers of the sixteenth and seventeenth centuries gave the name to first books for children. After 1600 the main purpose of the primer became educational.

To this class belonged *The New-England Primer*, rightly called "The Little Bible of New England." Sold first by Benjamin Harris at the London Coffee House in Boston, it went through many editions and was widely used for a period of one hundred and fifty years. From its small, ill-printed pages children learned to read, learned, too, from its shortened version of the Westminster Catechism what they were to think on matters of religion. The crude woodcuts with which it was illustrated must have put it into the picture book class, often the only book of its kind in a houseful of children. No wonder that its rhymed alphabet so adorned was early and easily memorized. Familiar and unaltered through many editions the lines ran,

> "In Adam's fall
> We sinnéd all."

But the variations in the couplets for later letters in the alphabet are multiplied by the changing state of relations with the mother country. Moreover, the other contents, too, differ in editions. After a while appeared the four lines used as an evening prayer by generations of children,

"Now I lay me down to sleep,
I pray the Lord my soul to keep.
If I should die before I wake
I pray the Lord my soul to take."

Later on the gentle "Cradle Hymn" and others by Isaac Watts were included.

At a time when the doctrines of fear and retribution so generally prevailed, it is a relief to find a man whose piety was tempered by gentleness and serenity, as was that of Isaac Watts. His name was a household word in New England. His hymnbook, from which the Psalms, often converted into doggerel and labored verse, were sung in all the churches, contained at least a half dozen majestic songs found in every hymnbook today. A young English clergyman without wife or child, he composed for the small daughters of his friend, Sir Thomas Abney, the volume of *Divine and Moral Songs* which became immediately popular in the colonies. Published in England in 1715, it ran through one hundred editions before the middle of the century. Altogether more than six hundred editions have been identified. Here appeared the still familiar lines, "How doth the little busy bee improve each shining hour," and "Let dogs delight to bark and bite."

Two books of great literature, unqualifiedly approved for children, the early colonists had in their often meager libraries. In the King James Bible they were the possessors of a rich store of varied writings which more than filled the place held today by fiction and poetry and history. Joseph and his Brethren, Samson and the Philistines, David and Goliath, Daniel in the Lions' Den—all these were wonderful stories for the boys and girls who heard them read over and over in the meetinghouses and at home. *Pilgrim's Progress*, too, was a book of wide popularity, one of the small group of great classics not written for children but taken over by them wholeheartedly. Simply by its contrast to the stern school of gloomy writing it was bound to appear a stirring tale of adventure and romance. A well-known passage in Benjamin Franklin's *Autobiography* records his pleasure in Bunyan. Franklin was a great reader and not at all satisfied with the religious books open to him. From Plutarch's *Lives* he drew much satisfaction, but he regretted in later years that he had in boyhood so few books to satisfy his thirst for knowledge. But if the supply was limited it was yet quite as good and quite as abundant as that available to children in England. Moreover, shortly before the Revolution the new era in children's books in both countries had set in with the kindly outflow from John Newbery's bookshop in St. Paul's Churchyard.

As the Puritan age passed, the element of entertainment appeared in chapbook form, to be had for a few pennies apiece. Franklin mentions his purchase of a considerable collection of chapbooks, but he does not mention names. We know, however, that Perrault's fairy tales, Cinderella,

Blue Beard, and the rest, as well as separate stories from the Arabian Nights, were sold in the little paper-covered leaflets that were the first form for books of amusement. *Robinson Crusoe*, published by Hugh Gaine in New York in 1774, was in chapbook format. Although abridged it yet told the adventures of the renowned hero on his uninhabited island. Dr. Rosenbach believes this may have been a Newbery reprint, as Hugh Gaine was not unlike John Newbery in that he, too, sold patent medicines and printed attractive toy books.

Anna Green Winslow, the Boston schoolgirl of Revolutionary days, noted in her *Diary* her New Year's Gift of 1772, the Bible, *Pilgrim's Progress*, *Gulliver's Travels* and the *History of Joseph Andrews*, abreviated [sic]. She also borrowed three of Cousin Charles' books, *The Puzzling-Cap*, *The Female Orators* and the *History of Gaffer* [Goody] *Two Shoes*. Plainly these were all fresh from London, as *Goody Two Shoes* and *The Puzzling-Cap* were not reprinted in America until a later date. The fashion to abridge adult novels to make them suitable for children had arisen. *Pamela, Clarissa Harlowe, Tom Jones, Gulliver's Travels* were all printed by Newbery among his little books greatly reduced in size for younger readers. Of the group, *Gulliver* alone has survived in the favor of those who buy books for boys and girls.

Goody Two Shoes, the most celebrated of John Newbery's inventions, was reprinted in Worcester by Isaiah Thomas, the first American printer not content with taking English books as they were. Practically everything he transplanted was altered to suit the American setting. Nor did Thomas seem to have any compunctions in making whatever changes seemed desirable, nor in adopting another man's work as his own. His life was an interesting one. He was a Boston boy, apprenticed at six years of age to Zechariah Fowle, a printer for whom he worked eleven years. When later he had secured his own establishment he became so obnoxious to the British forces in Boston by reason of his patriotic paper, *The Massachusetts Spy*, that the town became too hot for him. A few nights before the Battle of Lexington he packed up his presses and types and sent them across the Charles River and thence to Worcester. After the battle, in which he took part, he went to Worcester and resumed his printing.

The name of Isaiah Thomas will always be closely associated in literary history with that of John Newbery, whom he copied sedulously. All the Newbery successes were appropriated by Thomas, who was quick to give them a patriotic appeal by turning allusions to royalty into references to governors and Congress. The history of early children's books in Boston bears a close relation to the political situation in the Revolutionary period. John Mein— who opened the first Boston circulating library, advertised in 1765 as containing ten thousand volumes—was an importer of little books from Newbery's famous stock for children. Such books as *Giles Gingerbread* and *The Famous Tommy*

Thumb's Little Story-Book were sold at his "London Book Store." When the Non-Importation Agreement made English books for children unpopular in the years just prior to the Revolution, John Mein was marked as a loyalist and returned to England.

With the importation and imitation of Newbery books the tide of little books of amusement swept in. The titles are characteristic of the time: *Be Merry and Wise; or the Cream of the Jests and the Marrow of Maxims For the Conduct of Life. Published for the Use of all good Little Boys and Girls.* By Tommy Trapwit, Esq.; *The History of Giles Gingerbread, a little boy who lived upon Learning; The Wisdom of Crop the Conjuror; Nurse Truelove's New-Year's Gift.* Besides introducing *Goody Two Shoes* in an American edition, Isaiah Thomas naturalized *Mother Goose's Melody: or Sonnets for the Cradle,* in which he made a few changes though following Newbery's edition in the main.

On the whole, children could now procure a fairly varied supply of reading, if they had money for the purchase, and the price was generally low. There were the collections of riddles of which *The Puzzling-Cap* is an example. Always a favorite source of entertainment, such books are perhaps to be counted as games rather than as literature.

Then from the old French fairy tale Thomas produced a play, "The Beauty and the Monster," which appears something of an innovation. However, it was probably intended more to facilitate reading than for acting. More attention, too, was given to instruction about the animal kingdom. In *Jacky Dandy's Delight: or, the History of Birds and Beasts* we find numerous woodcuts accompanied by verses which usually point a moral.

> "The Bear in coldest climate lives,
>   Screen'd by his shaggy hair;
>   But boys may cold and hunger dread
>   Who naught for learning care."

No doubt such was the small volume that pleased Dicky Lee some years earlier when he wrote to his cousin, George Washington, that his father had brought him two pretty books full of pictures. "They have pictures of dogs and cats and tigers and elefants and ever so many pretty things," wrote Dicky.

Still the writers hid themselves in anonymity. Charley Columbus was responsible for one title, Tom Trip for another containing the same descriptions with different woodcuts.

Hugh Gaine and Isaiah Thomas brought over from England the illustrations by the Bewicks, which were not only far superior to what had been seen, but were also to prove the source of inspiration to an American artist of distinction. The work of Alexander Anderson, called "the father of woodcutting in America," is accounted nearly, if not quite, as good as the best woodcuts of Thomas Bewick. In the field of illustration alone, American work for children surpassed that done in England during the same period. From the press of William Charles at Philadelphia there was issued a series of square books with plain and colored engravings of great charm. The colors were frequently put on by children, each set down with a brush to engage in an occupation far more like play than work. Of course, the colored books cost more than the plain ones. We remember Robert Louis Stevenson's essay at a much later time, on the superior merits of "tuppence colored" over "a penny plain."

By the beginning of the nineteenth century there was no lack of books of amusement and instruction, but there was small indication of originality.   All follow English models, if they are not actually the work of English writers.

American producers were very faithful copyists, even in the matter of crying their wares. Newbery's rhymed advertisements were duplicated many times. Mahlon Day, the New York printer, proved especially ingenious in keeping his name before the youthful public by a variety of flourishes. A typical quatrain reads:

> "Some children for cakes are inclined,
>   Some buy a little barking Tray.
>   But don't forget there is food for the mind
>   In the books that are sold by M. Day."

After the sway of the strictly religious book was over the hand of the moralist was to rest heavily on books for children for many years. George the Third's long reign was drawing to a close when Maria Edgeworth began her career as a writer for children. The forces that shaped her course, the influence of Rousseau, the example of Thomas Day, her father's direction, are worthy of separate consideration. It is enough to emphasize here the importance of her contribution in dignifying writing for children. Her skill in the construction of plots, her sense of humor, her attention to lifelike detail, her ability to write well are all significant for their effect upon those who followed her. But Maria Edgeworth's crowning distinction is her power to create real children. For this alone she stands head and shoulders above her predecessors and contemporaries. With her name, realism in children's books has its beginning.

FROM ROLLO TO TOM SAWYER

II

OULD there be a wider gulf of separation between two types of book children than that between docile, earnest, literal, inquiring Rollo and mischievous, imaginative, harum-scarum, happy-go-lucky Tom? And yet this gulf was largely bridged in the fifteen years following the Civil War, that period of bad taste in architecture and house furnishings, of self-consciousness, of repressions and inhibitions. It is through consideration of the reading of New England children in the 1870's that we may trace some of the factors contributing to the greater freedom in the attitude toward children's reading. We shall discover a great fertility in the production of children's books, the first widespread awakening to the need of critical appraisal, the first wholehearted liberality toward children's tastes and interests, admitted without boundaries, without propaganda—in short, it was the beginning of a new era.

In *A Mid-Century Child and Her Books*, Caroline Hewins gives us a charming picture of the reading open to a child in a cultivated home in New England during the 1850's and sixties, when she herself was between the ages of five and fifteen. Miss Hewins counted the influence of the books that she read in those years so important that she later brought together in her library copies of as many as she could find to illustrate different phases in the history of children's books. Her early delight in the pleasures of reading, coupled with her lively remembrance of childhood tastes and native literary discernment, made her throughout life a warm champion of children and their books. Her own influence was wide and lasting, always to be felt by those who were privileged to know her personally and through those who were young when children's library work was in its infancy, an inspiration reaching far beyond her own personal circle and her own lifetime. The soundest principles of book selection for young people accepted today follow lines that Caroline Hewins laid down from the beginning of her association with the library in Hartford seventy years ago. With voice and pen she was always active in the cause of good books for children and her keen literary judgment, humor and pungent speech made her opinions highly valued by head librarians in library conferences and gatherings.

Early New England drew largely from old England the reading granted its children until well past 1850, but the children who began their association with books during the next two decades were destined to see a great change in the number of books designed in America for their special pleasure.

Those were the memorable years of the renaissance in the literary life of the six seaboard states—the golden age of American literature. If, in the 1870's, New England was declining from its pre-eminent position, many of the figures of that brilliant flowering were still living. Emerson was in retirement, it is true, but Longfellow, Whittier, Lowell and Holmes all were active with their pens. Parkman's great historical panorama was in process of unfolding. Hawthorne, with his unique imaginative powers, had not long been gone. Fathers and mothers who had felt the impact of this distinctive creative period could not fail to pass on something of a literary tradition to the children growing up in their homes. Those children accepted as an indisputable fact the importance of books in the lives of people—they had a respect for literature.

In Cambridge the little granddaughter of Jacob Abbott, later the author of *Molly Make-Believe*, averse to learning to read, yielded to the cajolery of the famous creator of the Rollo books who was summoned from Maine to see that she remained a dunce no longer. Poetry came to her straight from Longfellow who read her his most appealing verses. Then, as now, Longfellow was the children's poet, belonging as much to Maine as to Massachusetts. Children loved the

Norseland poems, *Hiawatha*, *The Building of the Ship*, *Paul Revere's Ride*, and other storytelling poems. From Whittier, too, came pictures of scenes familiar to country children, the schoolhouse by the road, the silence and wonder of a snow-storm on a farm buried deep in drifts, the chores of old-fashioned farmers' boys.

At Gardiner, in Maine, Laura Richards was reading to her children many of the books her mother, Julia Ward Howe, had put into her hands at Green Peace in South Boston. After *Mother Goose* and Lear's *Book of Nonsense*, she began to introduce a six-year-old to *A Midsummer Night's Dream*, taking first the fairy and clown parts, then filling in as the child became familiar with the lighter part. After that she went on to *As You Like It* and *Twelfth Night*. Lear's *Book of Nonsense* was published in England in 1846, and all over England children and grownups rocked with glee over the inconsequence of his taking rhymes. Walter De La Mare says that Lear Limericks are very different from "mere limericks." Those were fortunate American children who did not miss this nonsense in childhood. Mrs. Richards fed much poetry to her children, especially songs, ballads and heroic verse, for she herself would rather read poetry than eat her dinner any day. And the poetry dearest to her was the ringing kind "with bells and trumpets."

Other mothers delighted to read poetry to their children. There were excellent anthologies with poetry classified into groups—Poems of Home and Childhood, Poems of Sentiment, Poems of Patriotism, and so on. There were, too, the *Lays of Ancient Rome, Marmion, Ivry, Lord Ullin's Daughter,* Byron's sonorous lines,

"The Assyrian came down like a wolf on the fold
  And his cohorts were gleaming with purple and gold."

Of the collections for younger children, Whittier's *Child Life* satisfied gentle moods.

Little children could have the fine edition of *Mother Goose* containing music and admirably illustrated by H. L. Stephens. They had *John Gilpin,* with Caldecott's unsurpassed pictures, and Walter Crane's *Baby's Opera;* they had *Struwwelpeter,* which they never took seriously; they had *The Nursery* with its large type and simple stories. Though the name suggests an English household, this monthly magazine for the youngest was a dearly loved American periodical.

Within New England homes the favorites of an older generation stood on the shelves to tempt exploring eyes and minds, the Waverley Novels, with *Ivanhoe* and *The Talisman* affording vigorous substance for plays of knights and tournaments; Dickens, who had lately died, was full of odd characters to quote and imitate, but he could not be acted in the barn on a rainy day; Cooper, ah, there was plenty of theater for long Saturdays in the woods! His heroes were both of the sea and of the forest. Whether under the name of Leatherstocking, Deerslayer, Pathfinder, or Hawkeye, brave Natty Bumppo was always the ideal hunter and frontiers-

man, lean and sinewy, keen of eye, wise in the ways of Indians, long enduring, yet gentle and considerate, an American
to the core. His deeds made wilderness life alluring, for Indian warfare was not too remote from young people in
the 1870's.

History reading was held in high esteem in New England,
from the days when Abigail Adams wrote to her husband in
Washington, in the midst of the Revolutionary War:

> "I have taken a very great fondness for reading Rollins'
> Ancient History since you left me. I am determined to go
> through with it, if possible in these my days of solitude.
> I find great pleasure and entertainment from it and I have
> persuaded Johnny to read me a page or two every day,
> and hope he will from his desire to oblige me, entertain a
> fondness for it."

Johnny (John Quincy Adams) was then seven years old.

A boy of the 1870's, with a true love of books and ease in
reading, was not daunted by the size or length of a history,
for if it ran to three volumes he need not make so many
trips to the circulating library to take out Motley's *Dutch
Republic* or *John of Barneveld*, full of glowing adventure and
splendid heroes, or Prescott's brilliant *Conquests*.

Closer in point of time and closer in significance, as well
as easier reading, was *The Boys of '76* by Charles Carleton
Coffin. For did not the Revolutionary War begin right here
at home with General Gage and the Boston boys, the Sons of

Liberty, Lexington, Concord and Bunker Hill? Fierce and uncompromising was the anti-British sentiment aroused by this exciting book. Carleton's *Winning His Way* and his four volumes relating to the campaigns of the Army of the Republic made exciting reading, too, but were not so popular as *The Boys of '76*. The Civil War was not much farther away from children in the seventies than World War II is from children now. Written in the heat of conflict and passion, all these books were one-sided and prejudiced.

Along the New England seaboard, from which ships sailed forth over the Seven Seas, captained by fathers, uncles and grandfathers, geography was a living thing and no part of the world too remote to be interesting. For those young readers who could enjoy travel, Lady Brassey's *Around the World in the Yacht "Sunbeam"* afforded intimate glimpses of pleasant family life on a luxury yacht of long ago. Or, if one preferred exploration, there was noble Elisha Kent's account of his search for the lost Franklin expedition in the far North, and his *Arctic Explorations* when he discovered the Humboldt glacier. Boys and girls in bookish homes read with enthusiasm Stanley's absorbing accounts of his search for Livingstone and his experience tracing the course of the mighty Congo, which were almost the fresh news of the day in the 1870's. And wildly improbable, even sensational, as Jules Verne's books then seemed, they were good for the imagination in their anticipation of twentieth-century wonders.

Among the children's books inherited from an earlier generation Jacob Abbott's red-covered Rollo books were beginning to seem old-fashioned. They had no plot, incident followed incident, and the story ended when the author was ready to stop. Jacob Abbott never intended his books to be merely storybooks; he wanted them to be useful, to give substantial instruction and cultivate the power to think. But he knew and loved children and never talked down to them. He believed in treating them with respect and in sharing life with them. For little girls there was real pleasure to be found in the Franconia stories where they could join with Malleville and Mary Bell in the fun of going blueberrying or hear the incomparable Beechnut tell about the fabulous shipwrecks and icebergs seen on his father's voyage to America.

Except for Hawthorne's *Wonder Book* and *Tanglewood Tales* there was little of the imaginative handed down and that little had its origin abroad. Everyone knew Ali Baba, Aladdin and Sindbad even when others of the Arabian Nights tales were unknown. The Grimm Brothers' collection of folklore came to England in the 1840's and thence to America; *The Rose and the Ring* was written in the next decade; so, also, *The King of the Golden River*, which Laura Richards counted a lifelong joy, most precious of all children's books. Certain of Andersen's stories were being published for the first time in *The Riverside Magazine*.

George Macdonald's lovely spiritual fairy tales, brought

over from England, were accepted in homes where a strong evangelical atmosphere was less friendly toward fairy tales in general. *The Little Lame Prince* was dearly loved in those Victorian days and its moral was never even noticed. Besides Mrs. Mulock-Craik, who wrote it, another English woman was exploring the realm of imagination. Annie Keary, who had ventured to present to English children the Norse myths in the *Heroes of Asgard*, wrote a favorite story called *Little Wanderlin* which tells how a boy who never helped anyone was taken to Mrs. Calkill's wonderful house and there was turned into an elf. He traveled through the air and under the sea on a gull's back, learning to be sorry for his selfishness and antedating the adventures of Nils by some forty years.

The most important of all imaginative stories for children, *Alice in Wonderland*, published in 1865, crossed the sea early and later took its place in the juvenile section of widely distributed lists of good books. Happy the children in whose home it was a treasure.

Once having tasted at home the joys of reading, intelligent children felt compelled to supplement the family book shelves by borrowing elsewhere. Though as yet children's reading rooms in libraries were far in the future, New England was well supplied with circulating libraries, many of them supported by public funds. Often these had age restrictions, limiting borrowers to those over sixteen years. But children used their parents' cards as they do now and there were ways of circumventing the rules.

A library report of the period records that two small girls were observed by a vigilant official carrying away five books and holding them in such a way that it was evident a very small accident would throw some of the five volumes into the gutter. And another regretfully states that, "One boy sold his father's card to another boy, who lent it to a third who lost both books and card, but the three boys came to the Library and united to pay for the books lost."

There was one widespread agency which did cater eagerly to children; it was the Sunday-school libraries commonly flourishing in city, town and village. Few personal reminiscences of childhood reading in the first three quarters of the nineteenth century fail to mention the books brought home from the church schools.

While the weight of the Puritan sabbath had been measurably lightened by the 1870's there were nevertheless many homes in New England where children were not expected, or even allowed, to read on Sunday the books they could have on any other day of the week. Moreover, conventional observance of Sunday called for decorous inactivity in the long afternoon, leaving reading the only resource of boys and girls in the stricter homes, so in spite of inward rebellion, the Sunday-school library became their mainstay. As we trace the general and extensive use of these libraries it is important to remember that in this part of the world concern for children's reading grew, in the first instance, out of the Puritan emphasis upon the religious life of the child.

It was about 1830 that the American Sunday School Union, already in existence for some six years in Philadelphia, deliberately set out to create a juvenile literature for a public inadequately supplied, they felt, with suitable reading matter. In the next thirty years they actually produced a literature, widely read and greatly effective in developing the reading habits of a large part of the American people.

Four rules were set down to be followed by writers of books acceptable for publication by this organization:

(1) The book must be clearly and absolutely of a moral and religious character. (2) It must be graded and adapted to the capacity of the growing mind of the child. (3) It must be of a high order of style and fairly good literature. (4) The book must be American and for American children.

On this last requirement the Committee pointed out that there was no need to go abroad for subjects and scenes of interest; "American statesmen and benefactors, American forests, prairies and rivers, American prospects" might surely furnish enough subjects to make profitable and interesting reading for American children.

So far as I know, this was the earliest American attempt to set up standards for writing children's books. True, the rule that the book must be of a high order of style and good literature seems early to have lapsed with the emphasis placed more upon religious character. But while the books of the early years were often controversial, the Sunday School Union itself proved desirous of eliminating all denominational emphasis and by the 1870's books that had comparatively little actual religious teaching formed an increasing percentage of the Sunday-school library collections.

Aware that every child attending Sunday school expected to take home a book, and that this book was often read by several members of the family, some of the religious leaders began to be alarmed by the indiscriminate production of these library books; one a day and all the while increasing, they said. At the same time, secular publishers became conscious of the large and growing market over the country, and determined to enter a field in which appetites were so eager.

The Sunday School Union suggested, uneasily, that churches appoint their own reading committees of persons qualified to make wise choice of books for their own parishes, for they perceived the evils of unregulated purchase. Catalogues of Sunday-school libraries of the 1860's and 1870's are largely made up of colorless titles by unknown writers whose books cannot be recognized as belonging to authentic literature for children. It is no wonder that recommendations that the libraries be discontinued were common, or that some parents looked with disapproval upon books brought home on Sundays.

But fortunately, once fully conscious of the widespread circulation of books overloaded with precocious goodness, morbid piety and sickly sentiment, certain enlightened organizations took the matter vigorously and competently in hand. One of the most influential of these societies was the Ladies' Commission of the American Unitarian Society, in Boston, whose admirable lists, published and renewed in the years preceding the opening of children's rooms, were an invaluable aid to public libraries as well as denominational ones. In these excellent lists are to be found the names of books by established English writers for children, George Macdonald, Charlotte Yonge and Mrs. Craik, as well as a selection by Dickens and Scott. Widely used, these lists did much to overcome the flood of sentimentality which flowed so plentifully in the Elsie Dinsmore books and the less tearful stories by Pansy.

When during the 1870's the public library movement began its rapid development, the Sunday-school libraries no longer filled the place they had long enjoyed, except in rural communities where their popularity continued for several decades. Legislative authority for the maintenance of libraries by public funds, given in Massachusetts in 1848, spread over the New England states rapidly, with New Hampshire enacting such a law the next year. When the American Library Association was established in 1876, the

Centennial year, New England was fully prepared to join. Boston with its six branch libraries, then, was the first city in the country to organize a library system.

In Hartford, Miss Hewins had become librarian of the Young Men's Institute which later became the Hartford Public Library. Her swift disapproval of the type of books which many children were then reading took action in the preparation of unusual reading lists; her voice in favor of discerning criticism was one of decision and leadership.

Among other librarians who felt deeply the responsibility for the eager young readers was William E. Foster of the Providence Public Library, whose early paper on cooperation with schools is a landmark in that field. At Quincy the library trustees were deeply concerned with the subject, and papers by Charles Francis Adams and Josiah Quincy are sound reading today.

Meanwhile, the new freedom from the bonds of didacticism had brought on, here and abroad, the tide of adventurous fiction in which American writers proved to be highly prolific. Properly, this type of literature might be said to start with *Robinson Crusoe*, which has held its place all through the years, although it has in its original form a full share of religious passages. This was the first real book of the Connecticut Yankee, Governor Wilbur L. Cross, a country boy of the 1870's, who puzzled over the difficult passages in the uncut version, believing every word from cover to cover.

Next to Fenimore Cooper's books, Daniel P. Thompson's *Green Mountain Boys* had long held an honorable place in New England homes and libraries and was read by men and boys with a taste for stories from history. A truthful picture of pioneer days, it was written out of a lively sense of the Vermont struggle to keep its boundaries free from New York claimants and British oppression. Thompson's tales of Revolutionary heroes drew from the memories of those who had known the men and it was more truly a novel than a book written especially for young people.

Four Englishmen were in the forefront in establishing a pattern for adventurous fiction primarily for adults but also read by boys, at least twenty years before our period: Marryat, Kingston, Ballantyne and Mayne Reid, no one of whom was an armchair traveler. Captain Marryat was the earliest. He remains for this country the only one of the four whose books are wont to appear in new editions from time to time. Marryat's books have often a strongly religious and moral tone, but *Masterman Ready*, a castaway tale, and *Children of the New Forest*, drawn from history, have genuine story interest as well. *Mr. Midshipman Easy*, written out of his own experiences in the British Navy, was also popular.

W. H. G. Kingston, too, was in the British Navy before he wrote *Peter the Whaler* and *The Three Midshipmen*. Some of his books are full of details of animal life. *In the Wilds of Africa* fascinated quite young children with its tales about elephants, lions and gorillas.

Ballantyne wrote a number of trustworthy accounts of travel in the far North where his own fortunes had carried him, and several of his books were long on the shelves of children's rooms, as were those of Paul Du Chaillu.

As for Captain Mayne Reid, some of whose adventures with American Indians really took place, he belongs in both camps, the informational and the sensational. He had run away to sea and had his fill of Indian fighting. *Afloat in the Forest*, which continued as a serial in *Our Young Folks*, contains much detailed description about South American jungles and rivers. Laura Richards has testified that all she knew of natural history she learned from Mayne Reid whose dashing heroes were her delight.

Yet he was also one of the host of writers whose books were published by the Beadles of New York, responsible for the deluge of notorious paper-covered dime novels, which every New England boy knew it was a "Major Crime" to read. Beadle's Dime Books, Munro's Ten Cent Books, and subsequent series of Civil War stories, all flourished and waxed strong in the 1870's. By 1880, the dime novel business was a thriving industry, making fortunes for the manufacturers.

Edward S. Ellis, author of the Deerfoot series even now fondly remembered by Old Boys, was another dime novel writer with as many as six pen names. He began to write when he was hardly more than a boy himself and produced altogether over a dozen series of juvenile stories, as well as several respectable histories and biographies. He was at one time even a school superintendent in New Jersey. The Deerfoot series drew their inspiration from Cooper; they were bound books and are probably best remembered of anything Ellis wrote.

Oliver Optic, who was responsible for the issue of 116 volumes, in cloth bindings, not published by Beadle but by more reputable firms, was the pen name of a Boston teacher and school principal. His books were circulated freely and long by public libraries. In the 1875 catalogue of the Cambridge Public Library seven series by Optic are listed, and other libraries agreed in naming him as among the most popular fiction authors, whose works were read by men as well as boys and girls. Some contemporary reviewers called his stories pure and ennobling, "improving the taste and elevating the mind, while at the same time they stirred the blood and warmed the heart." Yet before his death his books were ruled out of most public libraries.

One need only turn the pages of *Outward Bound*, widely read long after its publication in Boston in 1872, to realize how little true criticism there was then, so far as children's books were concerned. In breathless one-line sentences, the career of a reckless youth on a school ship with many companions is expanded through page after page, punctuated with stilted speeches. The boys stole, they drank, they gambled, they had pistols, they even read "yellow covered novels," and they conspired to mutiny against the officers. The conversation of his young ladies was absurd.

When Billy Phelps, of Hartford, Connecticut, was twelve years old in 1877, he went to the Watkinson Library to take out one of Oliver Optic's Outward Bound series. Mr. Frank Gay, the wise head of the library, asked the boy why he read so much trash. Young Phelps replied that he read it because he liked it. After Mr. Gay had suggested that the boy read Shakespeare, a suggestion promptly resented, a bargain was struck between the two. The librarian proposed that Billy read one play by Shakespeare and if he did not like it, Mr. Gay would never ask him to read another and, more than that, he would keep the lad informed of every new book by Oliver Optic as it was placed on the library shelves. This seemed fair enough and the experiment began with *Julius Caesar*, which was read with great excitement and immediately followed by fifteen or twenty more of Shakespeare's plays. That William Lyon Phelps' catholic taste continued may be gathered from an entry in his journal, two years later.

"I read the entire book of Psalms today. This morning I finished *Jean Têterol's Idea* (by Cherbuliez) and in the afternoon and evening read two books of the Gunboat series."

Harry Castlemon, pen name of Charles A. Fosdick, seems to have been slightly less well known in New England than he was in the Middle States, but there are still men who think with nostalgia of *Frank on a Gunboat* and *Frank on the Lower*

Mississippi. The author claimed that the adventures of this series and of his other books really took place; and as he had run away from home to join the Navy during the Civil War, this may be true. His further claim that he had never met with one word of criticism seems a little less credible.

The name of Horatio Alger, one of the most widely read writers of boys' stories in the whole range of American literature, is a synonym for the success story. Whether or not his *Ragged Dick* and *Phil the Fiddler* resulted in putting an end to the exploitation of boys in the New York street trades, as has been claimed, his books have actually had a wide and possibly hurtful effect upon the reading tastes of countless young people. Supposedly an educated man himself, his writing was cheap and tawdry, his characters impossible, his plots repeated endlessly. Alger vulgarized high ideals and stressed the aim of life to be material success; his values were false; his moralizing, of which there purported to be much, was insincere because his own life was sordid.

Careful mothers along the New England coast who frowned upon sensational books gave a somewhat reluctant approval to the reading of books by Elijah Kellogg—reluctant because the scenes were often rough, the English faulty. But while the characters are wooden, the conversation unnatural, the stories are straightforward and honest with an infusion of robust orthodox Christianity, but never goody-goody or insincere, and full of scorn for meanness. Elijah Kellogg was a minister, the son of a minister who had been widely known and respected, and was himself a loved figure at Harpswell near Portland. Kellogg drew upon the pioneer history of Maine soon after the Revolutionary War for his material, and his accounts of the hardships and perils of the early settlers, the dangerous hazards of fishermen, the rugged business of building a home in the unbroken forests, are authentic, deriving from his own family traditions and personal knowledge. The pictures Elijah Kellogg gives of the early fishing industry show the actual practice of the times, while the achievements of his gigantic leader, Lion Ben, were derived from legends of the deeds of valiant heroes of the Maine coast. It is the character of the writer shining through his books that makes the Elm Island and Pleasant Cove stories better than other series of the period, though as in the others, six books about the same persons tend to become rather thin.

Amid the crowd of clay figures who were moved about like puppets on the stage of Optic, Alger and Company on battlefield, shipboard or in the city streets, the figure of Tom Bailey has a lonely distinction. Yet, if you would know what boy life in New England was really like in the 1870's, you have only to turn to *The Story of a Bad Boy* for what amounts to an historical photograph. The snowball fights on Slatter's

Hill, carried out with military strategy and fury, the Fourth of July celebration when the old stagecoach was burned, the club initiation with its mysterious trappings, these were all a part of New England boyhood.

Tom Bailey, as he said himself, was not a very bad boy and there are no lurid unrealities in his narrative. Probably if events were too much like everyday life to capture the multitude, the unexaggerated happenings were so true to life that they were enjoyed. Essentially a true portrait, the book stands as the most enduring work of Thomas Bailey Aldrich, who was moved by an artistic, rather than an educational or merchandising, impulse to tell in a charming style what he knew about boys.

Tom Bailey was appreciably closer to New England boys than was Tom Brown, whose school days at Rugby were obscured by talk of fags and English class distinctions which seemed remote from American public school experience. But, of course, there were some good fights in the story.

With far more genius than was displayed by Thomas Bailey Aldrich and Thomas Hughes, Mark Twain reached back into his memories of young Sam Clemens and gave the world Tom Sawyer—no period picture but the figure of the eternal boy. Although it was written in 1876, few New England boys knew Tom Sawyer before 1880. Even then Mark Twain's riotous humor was scarcely appreciated. It was an exceptional public library where Tom Sawyer was allowed in the hands of children; and that Miss Hewins listed it among boys' books in her epoch-making book list of 1882 was one of the marks of her liberal librarianship.

While boys would seem to have fared more lavishly than their sisters in our period, the girls were by no means neglected by the publishers. Girls read boys' books then, as they do today, and it was well that they did, for even when such books were poor they were more vigorous as a whole than stories for girls. Many wholesome minded girls scorned Martha Finley's endless series about Elsie Dinsmore and set her down as the tiresome prig she was. But they often reveled in *The Lamplighter*, that amazingly popular novel of a generation earlier, which described vividly the degradation of the poorer sections of Boston as seen by hard-working Gerty. Turned out of doors in a blinding snowstorm as a child, Gerty lived to heap coals of fire upon the heads of her most unworthy acquaintances. Secretly, too, some girls luxuriated in the sentimental, self-sacrificing pages of *Tempest and Sunshine* and *St. Elmo*.

For little girls there was one beloved author whose habit of continuation took shape in four sets of six little books in a box, each bearing the name of the leading child character. Sophie May was not given to overmuch moralizing and she made a real effort to bestow individuality upon her children —Prudy, Dotty Dimple, Flaxie Frizzle and Flyaway—all pet names. The incidents in the uneventful lives of the Parlin children are those commonly found in books for little girls, accidents and misunderstandings, mischievous pranks and willful disobedience, the marriage of a favorite aunt, a visit to New York. It is hard now to grasp the reason for the widespread affection for these books until we contrast the children in them with the children of earlier stories. Then it becomes evident that Sophie May made an effort to get away from the type of impossibly exemplary children, and attempted to give personality to her children and draw them as they are, in good moods and in bad.

In an unusual article on children's books, written while Sophie May's books were being published, the sober and scholarly *North American Review*, mouthpiece of New England's most dignified literary circle, waxes enthusiastic about the author, declaring :

> "Genius comes in with Little Prudy. Compared with her all other book children are cold creations of literature only; she is the real thing."

That was the viewpoint of an adult who found quaintness and tenderness, drollery and charm in children's original sayings, in baby talk, grammatical mistakes, teasing and spoiled ways, which are often funny to grownups, but hardly the best reading for children. Here is Dotty Dimple musing: "I know I don't ought to. I'm a goin' to do wicked and get punished, but I *want* to do wicked and get punished. I've been goody till I'm all tired up."

Even boys sometimes read Sophie May's books. Robert Morss Lovett, a Boston boy of the seventies, a devotee of

J. T. Trowbridge, with a zeal for military history, one who grew up to do some writing of his own, tells of seeing the sets at a neighbor's house, in a period of starvation. Listen to his admission:

> "It was a shameful thing for one who had recently enacted Deerslayer and the Young Engineer even to look at such books and I averted my eyes; but in the evening, with home lessons done and time heavy I bribed my sister to go across the street and borrow *Little Prudy's Captain Horace*—the military title taking off something of the curse. And once drawn in I read the whole lot—they were so small that two or three a day wasn't much—and I fell for them all, all the heroines I mean—sedate Susie and patient Prudy and dashing Dotty Dimple—my first love. Flaxie Frizzle never made a hit with me, somehow."

But it is hardly fair to credit Sophie May with only the Prudy and Dotty Dimple books. Her *Quinnebasset Girls* with others in the Quinnebasset series for older girls were natural, lifelike stories comparing favorably with similar books today.

While the younger girls were still happy with Little Prudy, a more truly American story came from the press of Roberts Brothers to remain a children's classic for eighty years—*Little Women*, with its chronicle of the March family in all their endearing reality, their fun and their cheerfulness, their sorrows and heartaches. "The press generally commends it highly, and the young folks write expressing admiration," her father, Bronson Alcott, noted proudly in his Journal. "She is among the first," he wrote, "to draw her characters from New England life and scenes, and is more successful, in my judgment, in holding fast to nature, intermingling less of foreign sentiment than any of our novelists. Her culture has been left to nature and the bias of temperament and she comes to her pen taught simply by an experience that few of her age have had the good fortune to enjoy—freedom from the trammels of school and sects."

With what good courage Louisa Alcott undertook to admit her readers into the precious home circle we know from her own words. The years have paid generous tribute to her unselfishness, for no other American story for girls has reached a wider circle, no other heroine has been so well loved as dear, honest, open-hearted Jo March, best drawn because best known by Louisa Alcott.

Boys as well as girls read this book, too. Billy Phelps confided to his journal that he thought the book spoiled by not having Jo marry Laurie. "I won't marry Jo to Laurie to please anyone," Miss Alcott had told *her* Journal.

Miss Alcott with five other books following *Little Women* during the 1870's was not the only writer whose realistic stories of American girls exemplified the new kind of writing. Even before *Little Women* was published, two books by ⌊Mrs. A. D. T. Whitney brought natural young people before the girls of New England—*A Summer in*

Leslie Goldthwaite's Life and *Faith Gartney's Girlhood*. Mrs. Whitney was a good storyteller with a sense of humor and a gift of characterization which she called readily to service. Her books had a religious tone, which made them among the best acceptable to the stricter Sunday-school library committees, where Miss Alcott's were not. She included pleasing descriptions of New England country life and activities and yielded no more than Louisa Alcott to the temptation of writing long series. Susan Coolidge, with impetuous, lovable, mischievous Katy, and Elizabeth Stuart Phelps Ward, with the Gypsy books, were long to be found on the shelves of children's rooms, each with a popular boarding school story to her credit. *Nelly's Silver Mine* by Helen Hunt Jackson opened the eyes of many girls to the mining country of Colorado.

We were still in the magazine era in the 1870's. Some of the best American magazines for adults, the *Atlantic*, *Harper's Magazine*, the *Century*, were read under the kerosene lamps all over our region, and children dipped into them frequently. It was after the close of the Civil War that a change came over the periodicals intended for children. The double columns of *Merry's Museum*, to which Louisa Alcott had sent many short stories, was abandoned and a more friendly page was introduced.

True, *The Youth's Companion*, in form more newspaper than magazine, continued to go into New England homes everywhere. It had belonged to the whole family for a generation, providing a weekly stimulus to the moral and mental life of different ages, though its original stated aim was to entertain children and insensibly instruct them, occupy leisure hours and turn them to good account, warn against the ways of transgression and allure to those of virtue and piety. As time went on the religious element became less pronounced, but always *The Youth's Companion* kept its definite view as to what was healthy and moral for children, rejecting both love-making and killings as unsuitable.

Over the years this paper contained special articles by famous men from Wilkie Collins to Kipling, its feature pages of anecdotes afforded many a hearty laugh, its serial story kept up the suspense from week to week. It was in *The Youth's Companion* that one of the earliest series of hunting and camping stories, those by Charles Asbury Stephens, held boys absorbed in the 1870's.

"Children have too much reading and the fault is not theirs but their elders," wrote Horace E. Scudder, in the first issue of *The Riverside Magazine*, in 1867. Under one of the two most discriminating editors a children's magazine has ever had, this fine periodical ran its short course of four years, marking a new age in such publications. For although he felt that there were too many books for children, Mr. Scudder wisely saw in the abundance a movement that could not be checked but could be studied and influenced, an abundance from which selection should be made under high criteria of values, set by those who cared for the growth of children's minds.

Books placed before children should not be confined to literature expressly prepared for them, said Mr. Scudder; they need have no age limit, they need not be new, and they may best be introduced by reading aloud in the home. His informal notes about reading, addressed to parents, and running through the first two years of *The Riverside Magazine*, are full of wisdom. He undertook then to arouse in children an interest in great writers, Shakespeare, Plutarch, William Blake; he called attention to new English books, printed Browning's *Pied Piper of Hamelin* with a memorable illustration, reprinted certain old ballads, all the time encouraging the foremost writers of the day to write for his magazine and the best artists to make pictures for it.

To Horace Scudder American children owed a fresh introduction to Hans Christian Andersen, for each year of the *Riverside* was enriched by one or more of his delicate fairy tales, several being written especially for American readers. Scudder's sympathy and love for children gave him a peculiar kinship with the poet artist.

The magazine was brightened, too, by Frank Stockton's playful fancy as it showed itself in that charming group of tales about the fairy youth Ting-a-ling and his friend the good giant, embroidered with the gentle humor and curious surprises that make Frank Stockton's work unique. He was to become assistant editor to Mary Mapes Dodge when *St. Nicholas* came into being, bringing to his editorial task his bubbling vivacity, his exuberant fancy and lightness of touch, combined with his sane, kindly philosophy.

Behind the ideals of *The Riverside Magazine* lies the vision of the day when children would see themselves related to a wider world than that in which they were growing up. Peter Parley and Jacob Abbott dwelt upon the odd customs of other countries. Grace Greenwood's travel papers dealt with history mainly. Only two lasting books succeeded in giving children truthful and interesting pictures of child life in other lands—Jane Andrews' *Seven Little Sisters Who Live on the Round Ball That Floats in the Air* and Mary Mapes Dodge's *Hans Brinker*, both appearing in the 1860's. While neither of these was printed in *The Riverside Magazine*, they established a pattern for it worth following in their *Ten Boys Who Lived on the Road from Long Ago to Now* and *Land of Pluck*, respectively. Chapters from Bayard Taylor's *Boys of Other Countries* showed a similar friendly warmth.

For undiluted realism Mr. Scudder presented the Bodley family when that pleasantly inquisitive household moved a few miles into the country with all the fervor of a journey across the continent. While the Bodleys seem not too distant relatives of Rollo Holiday, their travels were punctuated by selections from general literature. At their best the Bodley books were considered only tame.

The last words in the *Riverside* are a calendar entry for December 31, "The Riverside Magazine for Young People died, 1870." Mr. Scudder did not expect to edit any more magazines for young people. He was sorry to give it up, but he did not give up, as long as he lived, an abiding interest in young people and their reading.

Handed down by older brothers and sisters, *Our Young Folks* was greatly enjoyed by the children of the 1870's. Living three years longer than the *Riverside*, it held an important place in the household before it was merged in *St. Nicholas*. Under the leadership of John T. Trowbridge *Our Young Folks* was full of good things. The Peterkins first made their bow to the public in its pages and in Abby Morton Diaz' *The William Henry Letters* a country boy, away at boarding school, told the family how he was getting on. He illustrated his letters, by his own hand, showing what was happening to a natural boy and his school friends. Nor was pure nonsense lacking, for "The Owl and the Pussy-Cat" and "The Duck and the Kangaroo" came to New England children through *Our Young Folks*.

Mr. Trowbridge brought to his editorship a genuine wish to give boys and girls only what would interest them rather than instruct. Out of his own boyhood in central New York he called up the memory of life along the Erie Canal, creating a real boy character in Jack Hazard. With his loved dog Lion, Jack became a favorite whose adventures were chronicled through several years of *Our Young Folks* and were

continued in the early numbers of *St. Nicholas*. One piece
of writing by Mr. Trowbridge stands out as a reminder of
the interval that separates the machine age from the 1870's
when typewriters were curiosities, telephones an unrealized
dream, automobiles and airplanes like wonders from Jules
Verne. This is the famous story poem, "Darius Green and His
Flying Machine," with its humorous account of a boy's
backyard experiment, written in country dialect and ending,

> "Wal, I like flyin' well enough,
> He said; but it ain't sich a thunderin' sight
> O' fun in it when ye come to light."

While with the advent of *St. Nicholas* the leadership in
publishing for children passed out of New England into
New York, the New England writers were well represented
among its contributors and the new magazine was distributed all over the country, and overseas as well, bringing
pleasure and enlightenment to a host of constant readers.
Thanks to the vision of Mary Mapes Dodge they had rich
treasure. Started in 1873, as a branch of the Scribner tree,
the first ten years of *St. Nicholas* are counted the most valuable in its history. Then appeared stories and poems that
have long held a central place in the permanent body of
American children's books.

Besides Frank Stockton, assistant editor during those
years, the list of important writers is a long one. Lucretia
Hale had more to tell about the Peterkins, about Elizabeth

Eliza and the problems of her piano, about Agamemnon's Career and about the little boys with their India rubber boots. There were nonsense verses by Laura Richards, "The King of the Hobbledygoblins," "Little John Bottlejohn." *Eight Cousins* and *Under the Lilacs* appeared, Susan Coolidge contributed *Eyebright*, Trowbridge sent in *The Young Surveyor*. *Boy Emigrants* was a favorite serial which grew out of Noah Brooks' own experiences when he and a friend struck out for the Far West, took up a claim in the territory of Kansas and then moved out on the overland emigrant trail to settle farther on.

Appealing to the same public as *St. Nicholas*, *Wide Awake* flourished for a number of years. It was published by Lothrop in Boston, had a fine large page and good type, but it was not so fully illustrated as *St. Nicholas*, nor was Ella Farman Pratt so gifted an editor as Mrs. Dodge.

The New England children who welcomed the mail which brought *St. Nicholas* in the 1870's made their first acquaintance with Howard Pyle in a set of animal fables; they met the Brownies in their initial adventures; they learned to like good pictures; they pored over Jack-in-the-Pulpit's wise advice, guessed the riddles, discovered the hobbies of children in distant states from their letters. Their horizons were widened, their reading tastes developed, their happiness increased by the beloved magazine which proclaimed that the new age in children's books had arrived.

"THE JUVENILE MISCELLANY"
AND ITS LITERARY LADIES
III

WHEN the first number of *The Juvenile Miscellany* was drawn from the press of John Putnam, of Boston, in September, 1826, John Quincy Adams, the nation's sixth president, was serving his first year in office to be followed by Andrew Jackson. The next eight years were to see the beginnings of modern America, not only in the growth of cities, the movement for free education, the introduction of manufactured goods, but in the signs of social reforms, temperance, woman's rights, the treatment of prisoners.

If we search for indications of these great stirrings in our first real magazine for children we shall be disappointed. And yet, perhaps, on later reflection marked evidence of humanitarian fires may be noted in the editor's stories of minority races and the physically handicapped.

Looked at today this recognized forerunner of modern periodicals for children is distinguished from its faltering predecessors by its unabashed Americanism, noticeable in the space given American history and biography and, no less, in the countless allusions to the American landscape so different from the English background of books hitherto available to children.

The stories printed in *The Juvenile Miscellany* are largely placed in New England, especially the countryside lying along the Charles or Merrimack Rivers, in the Berkshires and around Hartford. There the authors were at home, in the environment they knew best. Local pride is to be recognized, as well, in the description of the Quincy Railway, the first in the United States, built to draw blocks from the quarries for the shaft of Bunker Hill Monument.

Yet the magazine was by no means wholly provincial, for included in the contents are extracts from a journal written in 1818 enlarging upon the wonderful sights of New York and still further afield is a detailed description of the President's home in Washington. Short biographies of noted foreigners who had aided the young country, De Kalb, Kosciusko, Baron Steuben, alternate with sketches of such great national figures as Benjamin Franklin, William Penn and General Putnam and stories of the painter Benjamin West and the explorer John Ledyard. Incidents many times repeated in later publications first found a place in the pages of *The Juvenile Miscellany*.

Three numbers of the magazine are bound together in the small volume which covers the first year. Later, the numbers appear six times a year through 1836. Much of the writing in the early issues undoubtedly came from the hand of the editor herself. Hers was, unquestionably, the tale of two colonial children wandering from their home on Shawmut peninsula, soon to be called Boston, rescued and restored to their family by a kindly Indian woman. Hers, no less surely, "The Little Rebels," a play based on the now familiar episode of the Boston boys who visited General Howe's headquarters to complain of interference by British soldiers with their play on the Common. An amusing woodcut accompanies this historic scene.

In her introductory Address to the Young, printed in *The Juvenile Miscellany* for September, 1826, the editor asserts that she seldom meets a little girl, "even in the crowded streets of Boston, without thinking with anxious tenderness concerning her education, her temper and her principles." So broadened was this solicitude in her later maturity that Mrs. Child is best remembered as a philanthropist.

That Lydia Maria Francis, then in her twenty-fifth year, already the author of two successful novels, had launched a children's periodical was no secret to her friends, in spite of her modest anonymity. Lydia had always wanted to write. At the age of twelve she had the good luck to read Scott's *Waverley* and was so fascinated that she asked herself why she, too, might not become a novelist. Her daring ambition was encouraged by her older brother, whose books and conversation proved a valuable stimulus to her literary tastes.

Like the majority of American girls living in the first quarter of the nineteenth century, Miss Francis had little formal education but, thanks to her brother's books and the circle in which she was fortunately placed, she found means to satisfy an eager curiosity and thus acquire a well-stocked mind. With her innate good sense and fine intelligence, she took high place in the literary world of her day. Her father was a baker in Medford, Massachusetts, a man of solid worth with strong convictions against slavery and a genuine respect for intellectual pursuits. Two years after Lydia began her career as editor she was married to David Lee Child, a Boston lawyer who shared her zeal for literature and reform.

Called the foremost woman writer of the United States in the 1830's, Mrs. Child had a wide range of interests. Her first book, *Hobomok*, appeared anonymously when she was nineteen. Venturing into a field then untouched except for Cooper's first novel, *Hobomok* arrested the attention of readers because of its independence and enterprise in the use of a theme chosen from American history. Since imaginative writing which owed nothing to English sources was practically nonexistent in America then, this novel is generally recognized as the fruit of an article by John G. Palfrey in the *North American Review*, emphasizing the rich field offered novelists by American history.

Hobomok tells the story of an Indian youth and a daughter of Plymouth, bound together by marriage after her English lover was lost, separated on his return by the Indian's noble renunciation and subsequent disappearance. Stilted as the telling is, the book had significance by reason of the sincerity of its effort to picture the life of the colonists in a romantic and original fashion.

The reception accorded *Hobomok* led the way to other historical novels, *The Rebels*, dealing with the American Revolution and much later, *Philothea*, a tale of Greece in the age of Pericles in which a timid innocent maiden of matchless beauty moves stainlessly among the rich and worldly of her city. It must be admitted, however, that Mrs. Child's most popular work for adults was *The Frugal Housewife*, with its lessons in New England thrift, ways to save expense and waste nothing. This went into many editions. Throughout a long lifetime her pen was seldom idle, for she was always aiming to instruct her readers or to "sow some seeds for freedom, truth and humanity," always ready to champion the cause of the oppressed, the prisoner, the Negro and all persecuted races.

At the time Lydia Francis started *The Juvenile Miscellany* her work as a reformer was all in the future, her concern was simply to give pleasure and information to children. So she turned lightly from stories and plays to factual articles on coral reefs or gases, or propounded easy riddles and set home-spun puzzles. Nor would the paper truly belong to its time were the didactic element lacking. Brief dialogues appear on ethical themes, on "Keeping Promises" and " Memory," suited to youthful understanding. But while her composi-tions sometimes took a rhymed form, Whittier, her stoutest eulogist, admitted that she was no poet.

The first editor was not long dependent upon her own in-vention. Early in the history of the *Miscellany* she announced the reception of excellent contributions for which there was no room. Gradually, we find one or more initials at the foot of the contents. Mr. Child obviously lent his help from time to time and other initials are easily identified as those of well-known writers of the day.

Something of the nature of the books then approved in a well-to-do family living in a city may be gathered from a narrative entitled "Children's Books." In this story four children walking along Washington Street in Boston are discussing what they will buy with the two dollars their mother had given to each.

"'I shall go to Munroe and Francis to buy *The Pearl*,' said Mary, a tall pretty girl of fourteen, 'for it has eight beautiful engravings in it and a great many pretty stories.'"

She describes a picture and tells how the lady who signs L.H.S., in the *Miscellany*, has written a pretty piece of poetry about the flowers dressing up for a prize. She mentions *The Mirror*, and this brings out an exclamation from Alfred,

> " 'Oh, that *Mirror* was a proper pretty book. What a capital story that is about the old woman who was caught out in a snowstorm and dillydallied about till her poor children were frozen at home. I shall read all the stories that lady writes.' "

He decides to buy a little arithmetic for Henry at home, while Lucy plans to spend her two dollars for *The Juvenile Keepsake*, soon to be published by Carter and Hendee, of which she has seen some of the pictures and proof sheets at Aunt Maria's. Jane, who loves all of Peter Parley's books, resolves to buy his little *Geography*, as another gift for Henry, whose education evidently rests heavily on the minds of brother and sister. Both *The Juvenile Keepsake* and *The Pearl*, mentioned by these children, are among the Annuals receiving high praise in the *American Journal of Education* for January, 1830. Perhaps Aunt Maria wrote the reviews.

So smoothly did the *Miscellany* seem to pursue its way that the subscribers could scarcely have been prepared for the sad note of 1834, in which the editor bade a reluctant and affectionate farewell to the readers and requested writers to send no more contributions, because the magazine was about to be discontinued for lack of patronage. The reason is not far to seek. Such was Mrs. Child's intense activity in the unpopular anti-slavery cause that she had now become notorious. Barely a year had passed since the publication of her ardent "Appeal for that class of Americans called Africans," the first book against slavery to appear in America. She was numbered among the conspicuous leaders of the abolition movement. She was no longer acceptable in society and was dropped from membership in the Boston Athenaeum.

While her association with *The Juvenile Miscellany* is the principal factor entitling Lydia Maria Child to a place in the history of children's literature in the United States, she produced a number of juvenile books well liked in their day. *The Little Girl's Own Book* (1831) was one of the earliest examples of that large class of useful volumes of games and riddles, recipes and rules, designed to supply occupation for leisure hours.

In *Flowers for Children* and *New Flowers for Children* some of the favorite stories from the *Miscellany* were reprinted with an equal number of pieces written expressly for these books. The stories show affection for children combined with some understanding of their behavior. Without possessing much imagination they illustrate domestic manners and customs in New England during the first part of the nineteenth century. Titles like Little Jane, Little Mary, Little Emma, Discontented Dora, all characteristic of the period, were bound to make an appeal to young children.

It is in *Flowers for Children* and *New Flowers for Children*

that we find Mrs. Child's two most popular poems. Familiar
even now are the lines beginning

> "Over the river and through the wood
> To Grandmother's house we go."

This was originally entitled "The New England Boy's
Song about Thanksgiving Day." To match it there was
printed later a song by a New York boy in praise of Croton
water which runs in big pipes underground. These verses
recount the benefits of hydrants to dogs and horses. The
lines entitled "Who Stole the Bird's Nest?" by Mrs. Child
were long included in collections of verse for children and
still may be found in old-fashioned books.

Mrs. Child was the editor of Mrs. Tappan's collection of
short stories called *Rainbows for Children*. Two quite charming stories printed there show more imagination than was
commonly to be found in 1855, when they appeared. One,
based on a familiar folklore theme, concerns Fianna who
went around the world in search of a flask of golden water
which would heal the eyes of her blind sister. Fianna traveled
by turns on a whale, an ostrich and a camel among other
animals, real and fabulous, all of which, the writer says, gave
her an excellent opportunity to study natural history. She
was carried across the Pacific by a phoenix, across the prairie
by an eagle which had been summoned for her by two Indian boys. Walking and running at intervals, she rode on a
deer, a buffalo and, at the end, on a railway.

Another story, "Fanny's Menagerie," tells how a little girl is surprised one rainy day by visits from the animals who had supplied material utilized in some of the treasured possessions in her room. They came to take back their gifts and little was left to Fanny after the geese had taken her pillow, the horse her mattress, the sheep her shawl, the bees the wax from her doll's head, the whale the oil in her lamp, and the elephant her ivory basket.

If Lydia Maria Child left nothing of permanent value to enrich literature for children, her work may be counted that of a pioneer who had the courage to forsake English models and write for American children in terms of their world. Breaking a pathway toward freedom from heavy-handed didacticism, her magazine was truly a beacon for others.

A fresh series of *The Juvenile Miscellany* was projected immediately after her resignation, under another editor, long a valued contributor, now willing, with Mrs. Child's friendly approval, to carry on where the first editor had laid down her task. After the change, as before, the American scene was given prominence. Early in 1835, a glowing description, accompanied by an engraved plate, did honor to the "great railroad which will in time run clear from Boston to Buffalo."

Far more diplomatic in her reforms, successful in furthering a number of worthy movements without antagonizing the public as Mrs. Child had done, Sarah Josepha Hale is inseparably associated with *Godey's Lady's Book*. As its

"Lady Editor" Mrs. Hale holds a definite position in the history of journalism in America, but her share in the promotion of children's reading was a less constructive one than that of the first editor of *The Juvenile Miscellany*. She would never have believed, however, that a certain contribution made over the initials S.J.H. in 1830 would call forth a spirited controversy, within a limited circle, one hundred years later.

America has, perhaps, never produced a set of child rhymes more widely known than the verses that tell about Mary and the lamb that followed her to school, except possibly Clement C. Moore's "Visit from St. Nicholas." There was something about Mary's pet which caught the fancy of little children and likewise the fancy of industrious makers of school readers. Was it the complete naturalness and absence of moralizing? Whatever the reason the simple quatrains were read and sung and quoted by innumerable American parents after they were printed in the *Miscellany*.

That very same year the verses found a place in Mrs. Hale's own book, *Poems for Children*. Nobody knows which was the earlier date. Little heed to sources was given in those days of unstinted borrowing, so Mary's Lamb was printed anonymously in various school readers which gave it wide distribution. Among those books was McGuffey's Second Reader, that prime favorite over a generous section of the United States where it is still fondly remembered.

Not until after 1870 was the claim made by Mrs. Mary

Sawyer that she was the heroine of this poem written by a certain John Roulston who had died some fifty years earlier.

Now it is not improbable that more than one little girl living on a farm had a teachable pet lamb who followed her to school and nobody knows how Mrs. Hale heard the story. But *Wide Awake* magazine came to her support printing, in 1879, a letter from Mrs. Hale who was then living. Her letter states unequivocally that she was truly the poet, having written these and other verses at the request of the well-known composer, Lowell Mason, for him to put to music. There would seem to be no reason to doubt Mrs. Hale's word, as the evidence is all in her favor, had not the rival author been honored by Henry Ford on a bronze tablet in Sudbury. So visitors to his New England village are prone to accept this tablet on a little red schoolhouse, moved from Sterling to Sudbury by Mr. Ford, as proof that John Roulston, not Sarah Josepha Hale, wrote the poem about Mary and her lamb.

The fourteen-year-old girl of the family mentioned earlier, who bought books on Washington Street, expressed special admiration for a poem in *The Juvenile Miscellany* about the flowers dressing up for a prize, written by the lady who signed her contributions with the letters L.H.S. The subject indicates that it was one of the host of imitations of Roscoe's *Butterfly's Ball*, so popular in England at that time. Certainly it must have had some inspiration from outside, for it was far removed from the customary style of a writer whose effusions generally carried a weighty load of morals or were edged with mourning over an early death.

The Juvenile Miscellany was, no doubt, favored in presenting to its readers the work of Lydia Huntley Sigourney, the Sweet Singer of Hartford, a writer so popular that editors and publishers vied with one another to obtain her prose and verse, paying liberally for both. Among the periodicals and annuals published during the third and fourth decades of the nineteenth century there were few from which her sentimental outpourings were missing. Gathered from different magazines some of her verses were printed in her two volumes, *Poetry for Children* and *The Child's Book*. They dripped sweetness and emotion, reflecting the taste of a great body of adults in the age of sensibility. Only rarely, if ever, could they have given pleasure to a child.

Mrs. Sigourney's own life story is one her ardent readers must have loved. Daughter of a humble Connecticut gardener, patronized by a wealthy widow to whom she devoted her early years, marrying a prosperous merchant, rising from poverty by the aid of a facile pen, sought after as a distinguished "poetess," hers is indeed a success story of full dimensions.

Meatier food for children's minds was offered by Miss Leslie, of Philadelphia, another regular contributor to the *Miscellany*. Her stories, frequently published in *Godey's Lady's Book* or *Graham's Magazine*, were enjoyed by young girls since they were bright and entertaining, but though she enlivened the contents of *The Juvenile Miscellany* with an element from outside New England, she has left no trace on children's literature. She wrote of dolls as magnificent effigies, of richly caparisoned rocking horses and of the tempting delights of the confectioner's art "that have made Philadelphia famous as the city of cakes and pies."

Eliza Leslie was the sister of Charles Leslie, the American artist who lived long abroad and painted, among other portraits, one of Sir Walter Scott for George Ticknor, of Boston. She traveled with her brother. Her stories contain descriptions of scenes in Europe and, in her own Annual, *The Violet*, they are often illustrated with engravings by artists of wide reputation. Following Mrs. Child's lead Miss Leslie edited, in 1831, the *American Girl's Book* devoted to handiwork and pastimes.

Still another important contributor had a share in making *The Juvenile Miscellany* a representative publication. The qualifications of Catharine M. Sedgwick as an author for children were based not only on her affection for her own nieces and nephews, who looked to her for much of their entertainment, but also were rooted in a childhood love of books and a long association with the best in English. An established novelist, she belonged by birth to a cultivated circle in the Berkshires where Cooper and Bryant were frequent guests and to a home where reading aloud was habitual. When Catharine Sedgwick was eight years old her father insisted that she listen quietly while he read to older members of the family from Shakespeare, Hume and other English classics.

Before becoming one of the lights of the *Miscellany* Miss Sedgwick had published *The Travellers*, her first story for children, relating the experiences of a young brother and sister on a visit to Niagara with their parents. This was followed by other books mostly about New England, truthful and unaffected. *Hope Leslie* and *Redwood* were among her most widely read books. She praised the good and virtuous, contrasted the lot of the rich man with that of the poor but honest worker and stressed the beauty of character. Following this pattern her stories for the *Miscellany* served their purpose and have been forgotten.

Interspersed with the prose and verses of these foremost writers, *The Juvenile Miscellany* gave space to the verse of prolific rhymesters like Hannah F. Gould, of Newburyport, and Anna M. Wells. It printed letters from the South where Caroline Howard Gilman had moved from her Boston home. No other early magazine for children reached so wide an audience, none commanded the assistance of so many prominent persons of that time. There is good reason for it to be counted as a landmark in American literature for children.

PETER PARLEY

IV

O N a certain day in May, 1824, a young American who had been exploring the druid circle at Stonehenge and gazing reverently upon the lofty spire of Salisbury Cathedral took postchaise for a small village ten miles out of Bristol to call on a lady. He was not insensitive to the charm of the countryside, with its wide valley sloping to the Bay of Bristol, framed in the distance by the Welsh mountains, but his was not a poetic nature and the fragrance of spring in England was simply a cheerful prelude to the high moment of his grand tour.

Young Mr. Goodrich was in his early thirties at the time. Miss Hannah More, whose home at Barley Wood he was approaching as to the shrine of a divinity, was nearly eighty. Some six months earlier Mr. Goodrich had landed at Liverpool from an ocean so stormy that he thought it would be not only his first voyage but his last. Like other travelers he was to forget his unpleasant experiences after a few weeks ashore, and to enjoy thoroughly his European pilgrimage across England and France, into Switzerland, Germany and Holland, leading up to a return to England and this crowning event, so long anticipated, now to be realized.

The orderly young man noted with approval the neat gravel walks around the vine-covered cottage under its thatched roof. As his eye followed them he discovered a monument to the great John Locke, who was born many years before in a house still to be seen in the village. It seemed to the American visitor a spot twice blessed.

The little old lady of Barley Wood was physically frail and infirm, but her mind was still active. Dressed in a dark red bombazine gown, with hair "slightly frizzed and lightly powdered," she was plainly not above a care for her personal appearance. She inquired for Mrs. Sigourney and other friends in America. Goodrich told her of the inspiration he had drawn from her books, especially from *The Shepherd of Salisbury Plain*, which seemed to him hardly inferior to the Bible narrative of Joseph and his brethren; he told how from this highly moral tale he had received his first glimpse of the joys of reading, how great a benefactor to the human race he felt her to be.

What was she really like, this woman whose writings so widely and genuinely influenced readers in the England and America of her day? Her life seems to have had two quite distinct chapters. All the latter part was devoted wholly to improving the condition of the poor and to the spread of evangelical religion. To these ends she wrote innumerable tracts and books with simple moral lessons, extolling the virtues of honesty and piety, acceptance of one's lot, kindness, faithfulness to duty and a cheerful spirit. The child who was thankful when she remembered "What must poor people do who have no salt to their potatoes" was the daughter of the Shepherd of Salisbury Plain.

Hannah More's portrait, painted by Opie when she was much younger, shows a face of great sweetness, small regular features, fine dark eyes under a crown of abundant hair dressed high in the exaggerated style of the period. There can be no doubt that she possessed great charm in her youth.

One of the brilliant circle surrounding Dr. Johnson, she was an intimate friend of David Garrick and his attractive Viennese wife, who had given up her career as an admired dancer to marry the great actor. It was as a successful playwright and poet that Hannah More was welcomed into the intellectual society of the eighteenth century. A Blue Stocking, she was counted an ornament to the lively conversation parties attended by the Garricks, Sir Joshua Reynolds, Lady Mary Wortley Montagu, and the rest of the eminent circle. She looked up to Dr. Johnson with reverence, flattered him with admiration, and enjoyed with him a friendship similar to that bestowed upon another witty and graceful young woman, Fanny Burney.

Alas, it is only the curious, intent upon recreating the past, who would consider her writings worth attention today, for save the sincerity of their moral purpose they have little to praise. She had nothing of Fanny Burney's liveliness and wit, nothing of Maria Edgeworth's skill in plot or able delineation of character.

Although Hannah More did not write for children, many of her later books fell into their hands. Intended for the simple uneducated masses whom she hoped to elevate by means of moral tales, they had given Mr. Goodrich, of Connecticut, the germ of an idea which developed rapidly after his memorable visit to Barley Wood. Through his conversations there he was strengthened in his belief that facts could be made more interesting than fiction to children. He resolved to undertake the task of proving this by the production of suitable books containing only facts.

About three years after that visit, in 1827, there was published in Boston a little square book bearing the title, *Tales of Peter Parley about America.* It was the first use of a pen name, happily chosen and destined to become famous. It was, as well, the beginning of the flowing stream of books made in America, designed especially for the benefit of American children. When they were read at home or in the one-room schoolhouses over the country the names of familiar birds and trees, the mention of local rivers and towns gave a homely quality to the pages. These were things boys and girls had heard about.

For the next five years Peter Parley devoted himself to writing without revealing his identity, until the indefatigable

Mrs. Hale discovered and divulged the secret. Other small square volumes followed in rapid succession: *Tales of Peter Parley about Europe, Africa, Asia* and other countries, *Peter Parley's Tales about the Sun, Moon and Stars* and other books, sometimes several in a year. The thin square volumes which were Parley's *Geographies* were counted treasures of great value in remote country places. Marvelous pictures opened the world to eager eyes and revealed wonders hitherto undreamed of, Eskimo houses, caravans in the desert, strange animals like camels and elephants, never failing sources of delight to minds hungry for knowledge.

From the didactic school, then dominant in England, these books drew their full share of moralizing, but they breathed a fresh spirit of independence and complacent Americanism. As Peter Parley observes in his *Book of the United States:* "If therefore you were to visit foreign lands, you would meet with many curious manners and customs which you do not find in this country, and you would probably return satisfied that we are a plain, commonsense people, living on terms of great equality with each other, and more distinguished for general intelligence, simple manners, and a good opinion of ourselves than anything else."

The author of the Peter Parley books, Samuel Griswold Goodrich, is seldom thought of except by his chosen pseudonym. Born into a well-known Connecticut family, in 1793, he received the usual rural schooling of his time. His father was a Congregational minister in the village of Redfield, with a farm of forty acres to be worked on week days and made productive enough to support a family. In *Recollections of a Lifetime*, the son has drawn a realistic and entertaining picture of his home and the primitive hard-working community over which his father presided. The country towns of New England in the opening years of the nineteenth century harbored many shrewd odd characters, fit subjects for humorous anecdotes or legends, and memories of these are to be found in Goodrich's *Recollections*. Then the heroes of the Revolutionary War still lived to spread their patriotic tales among the boys and girls of the village and young Samuel lent a ready ear to these fragments of American history.

Farm life had little interest for the boy who possessed both the aptitude for mechanics, so often seen in New England, and a taste for intellectual pursuits. Passing through terms of storekeeping and bookselling, he became a publisher in Hartford and in Boston, where as author and editor he was responsible for one hundred and seventy books. By wide reading he fitted himself to associate with men of affairs and became State Senator. Shortly before the upheaval of 1848, he served as Consul at Paris when some of the Parley Tales were translated into French.

Looking back at his boyhood as he grew older, Peter Parley undoubtedly read into his memories the theories on children's literature which he had evolved in a lifetime. Up to his tenth year he had read but little outside his school books and *The New-England Primer*. Perhaps his introduction to Mother Goose as late as that accounts for his thinking the rhymes merely silly and always afterward scorning them for all children. Generally regarded as unimaginative, he must have been quite the opposite as a child, since he thought "Red Riding Hood" was true and was filled with horror by the tales of "Jack the Giant-Killer" and "Bluebeard."

When he was about twelve years of age he read *Robinson Crusoe* with delight, then a translation of the *Tales of the Castle*, by Madame de Genlis, followed by Hannah More's *Moral Sketches* and *The Shepherd of Salisbury Plain*. These were the first books to rouse any enthusiasm. "I do not recollect," he says, "to have discovered before this time that books contained inexhaustible sources of instruction and amusement and all within my own reach."

Peculiar interest centers around the boyhood of this man because of its obvious bearing upon his chief claim to be remembered. Whatever his later beliefs about children's reading may have been, they were rooted in prejudices and impressions formed when he was himself a child. Because as a literal-minded boy his association with folk tales had been unhappy, he entered upon a crusade against everything fanciful or imaginative; because the little dame school at Ridgefield had neither histories nor geographies for its pupils, he multiplied their production for other schools. As he reflected upon the subject he imagined himself on the floor with children and wrote as he would have talked, working out his ideas with the design of enlarging the children's knowledge.

In the library of the elder Goodrich the boy found a considerable collection of books including folios in Latin, mostly on theological subjects, with a scattering of books in English. When once he had learned to read, Samuel dipped into a big book which happened to be in large print, reading whole pages aloud to himself, spelling out long words, fascinated by type and sound, although he could not understand a single word. This experience he later interpreted as an indication of what other children enjoyed.

The name of Peter Parley was rightfully attached to one hundred and sixteen books, but there were many more, purporting to be his, published at home and abroad far up into the nineteenth century. The Original Peter Parley, as he called himself in capitals, certainly suffered much from the pirating of his books when they were greatly in vogue. He also complained bitterly of the "spurious Parleys." At the time Peter Parley began to write for children few textbooks were to be had; history, as such, was not taught in the schools; Noah Webster's "blue-backed" speller of renown still served as reading book in New England; the comprehensive series of McGuffey readers had not yet appeared to supply literary satisfaction to other parts of the United States. As soon as the school reader idea became financially profitable the five elementary books by Goodrich competed successfully.

The diligent producer declared that his object was "to make nursery books reasonable and truthful and thus to feed the young mind upon things wholesome and pure instead of things monstrous, false and pestilent." Confident that he alone was right in his characterization of old folk tales, he fiercely defended his theories against all opponents who believed in the value of the imagination. His quarrel with Sir Henry Cole forms an amusing chapter in itself.

Old Peter Parley followed the device of taking his readers on an imaginary journey and describing the experiences they were likely to have and the kind of people they would meet. Often he told his story in the first person, interspersing anecdotes and incidents in the style later employed by the authors of the Bodley books and the *Zigzag Journeys*. His books vary in quality, but the best ones are not dull, for the writer selected his material with an understanding of children's tastes, introducing unusual happenings sure to hold attention. There were pictures, too, crudely illustrating scenes in the text and adding greatly to the popularity of the volumes. He took a hand also in the magazine business and for about twelve years *Parley's Magazine* was planned by him but edited by others because of Goodrich's serious eye trouble. Quite frankly, Goodrich admits that he had help in his large enterprises, particularly in the preparation of the histories. Among the young writers contributing to the series pompously termed *Parley's Historical Compends*, easily the most distinguished was Nathaniel Hawthorne.

Goodrich edited, too, *The Token*, notable member of the family of annuals in the period of their greatest success. Among its contributors were numbered Longfellow, Hawthorne, Oliver Wendell Holmes and other writers, then almost unknown in the world of letters ruled by Cooper, Irving and Bryant.

As American Consul in Paris soon after the middle of the nineteenth century, Samuel G. Goodrich added to his reputation abroad as well as at home, so it could have been no surprise to his countrymen when he was singled out for a new honor toward the close of his life.

It was on a platform at New Orleans that the chairman of the meeting, speaking before a large crowd gathered to pay their respects to Samuel Griswold Goodrich, greeted the distinguished guest as "a blessed benefactor to the youth of the rising generation, as one who has emphatically earned the proud and endearing appellation 'L'Ami des Enfants.'" On this great occasion there were speakers from more than one country where the name of Peter Parley was highly regarded. A gentleman from Greece declared that Peter Parley's works had found a welcome in that classic land, another from England bore witness to the admiration they aroused all over Great Britain, while it was common knowledge that they had been translated into French. Self-opinionated he was and inherently prosaic, yet there is something likable about Peter Parley. He was honestly anxious to give good reading to children, but he was incapable of seeing worth in anything except the purely factual. Notwithstanding, a whole generation loved his books and found many of them amusing, gaining from them at the same time a wider view of the world and its people. For the strong influence that he had upon the development of American children's books he seems as deserving to be called "the children's friend" as was the Frenchman Arnaud Berquin.

THE CHILDREN OF
JACOB ABBOTT

V

A T the famous Christmas party given to book people by Miss Muffet and the Spider, one of the favored guests according to Dr. Crothers who reported the occasion, was the youth Rollo.

"I always did like Rollo," said Miss Muffet. "I almost forget that he is a Youth sometimes. The nicest thing about him is that you always know what he means. He always tells you where he is and how he got there, without skipping anything that you ought to know. When he goes into a room, he goes through the door, opening and shutting the door just as you expected. He isn't at all like Humpty Dumpty. I don't think I ever knew two people more different."

Is anyone acquainted with Rollo except by hearsay, now? Yet for many years he was one of the best known of all the characters created by Jacob Abbott, and the first truly American child in fiction to become popular.

If it was Peter Parley who started the stream of children's books with an American setting, it was the father of the four Abbott boys who first peopled them with natural lifelike children to work and play in American surroundings. No definite person stands out in any one of Peter Parley's books, but in those of Jacob Abbott there is a whole gallery of individuals whose names were household words in many families and whose blameless adventures held and delighted more than one generation of boys and girls.

Rollo is not a "Youth" but a very little boy when we first meet him. He plants corn in his garden and two days later, since it has not come up, he replants the garden with beans; he picks up chips.

> " 'When shall I learn to work, father?' said Rollo.
>
> 'I have been thinking that it is full time, now. You are about six years old, and they say that a boy of seven years old is able to earn his living.'
>
> 'Well, father, I wish you would teach me to work. What should you do first?'
>
> 'The first lesson would be to teach you to do some common, easy work *steadily*.' "

So Mr. Holiday proceeds in the most approved fashion to inculcate his young son with one of the sound New England doctrines of his time. In the twelve small volumes dealing with Rollo's childhood he is a real boy, quarreling with Cousin James over the building of a wigwam or keeping the best fruit for himself instead of giving it to Lucy; he is not a goody-goody as it is sometimes supposed. But his ordinary childish faults are always used by his parents as texts for instruction in right behavior.

True to the theories of the didactic school, the children in the Abbott books are allowed to reap the consequences of their own choices, though the fathers and mothers are far more understanding and sympathetic than those in the English books of the period. Wise counsel and patient explanations are furnished to guide children's actions and emphasis is laid upon the old-fashioned conception of duty. Jacob Abbott believed that moral conduct must be taught like walking and talking. He felt that industry and honesty were cornerstones of character; that the "amiable and gentle qualities of the heart" might be cultivated by books like his intended principally for entertainment.

The scenes of the Rollo books, the Franconia stories, and some of the others were laid in New England, in quiet country neighborhoods where respect for authority rules. Full of the details that children love, these books had a wide influence through all the middle years of the nineteenth century. The relation of a book to its generation is best measured against the literature that precedes it rather than what comes after. To children seventy-five years ago the Abbott stories were a new type. Then the familiarity of the setting delighted, the reality of the characters charmed, the store of useful information was remembered. Older people, too, gave their wholehearted approval to books from which so much was to be learned. An unnamed writer, much closer than we are to the heyday of the Rollo books, has commented amusingly upon them in the *North American Review* for 1866:

"These works are invaluable to fathers; by keeping always one volume in advance of his oldest son, a man can stand before the household an encyclopedia of every practical art. . . . In these paths of peace the principal guide, philosopher and friend is Jonas. . . . Jonas is an admirable creation—the typical New England boy, such a boy as every one of us has been or known. Steady, sensible, sagacious, not troubled with languor or imagination, he is always a wholesome companion who neither intoxicates nor misleads. Domestic and agricultural virtues adorn his sedate career. His little barn chamber is always neat; his tools are always sharp; if he makes a box it holds together, if he digs a ditch there the water flows. He attends lyceum lectures and experimentalizes on his slate at evening touching the abstruse properties of the number nine. Jonas is American Democracy in its teens; it is Jonas who has conducted our town meetings, built our commonwealth and fought our wars."

Jonas was the first of those remarkable young people,

generally portrayed in Jacob Abbott's stories as sources of universal knowledge, looked up to and revered by the younger children. Everyone who recalls the hero worship so touchingly given by little boys and girls to those somewhat older can see a reason for the invention of these model characters. Beechnut, Mary Bell and Rainbow are all equally intelligent and are all trusted implicitly by the grownups to shoulder the responsibilities of maturity and take complete charge of the younger ones. Though still in their early teens, they never disappoint their employers and friends, are never found wanting in resourcefulness and common sense.

When Rollo was twelve years old he was taken on a European tour, described in twelve volumes, very tedious to readers of the present day. He had then become a "Youth," who traveled through the countries of Europe with the satisfied consciousness of hailing from a land far superior to those inhabited by foreigners. He cannot at this stage escape the charge of being hopelessly priggish; he has proved a fit subject for caricature.

Far more successful in bringing a native of another land to America than in taking Americans abroad, Mr. Abbott enriched children's books by creating a French boy of genuine individuality in the person of Beechnut of the Franconia stories. This Swiss boy, originally from Geneva by way of Paris and Montreal, introduces a delightfully new element into the series, for he supplements the habitual round of rural joys with his inventiveness and gay spirits.

He plans unusual games, he makes unusual toys and gives them diverting names. With his precious picture of Paris, displayed on the wall of his bedroom, he has a starting point for stories of French life that entrance his listeners. All the arts of the storyteller are his. Who, having read it, does not remember his description of the voyage to America, with the famous example of embellishment, given to Malleville and her brother Phonny?

"'Shall I tell you the story just as it was, as a sober matter of fact, or shall I embellish it?'

'I don't know what you mean by embellishing it.'

'Why,' said Beechnut, 'not telling exactly what is true, but inventing something to add to it to make it interesting.'

'I want to have it true,' said Malleville, 'and interesting, too.'

'But sometimes,' replied Beechnut, 'interesting things don't happen; and in such cases, if we should only relate what actually does happen the story would be likely to be dull.'

'I think you had better embellish the story a little,' said Phonny; 'just a little, you know.'"

Then what a grand story of shipwreck and iceberg follows. Jacob Abbott was never afraid of using unfamiliar words in his stories if they expressed the meaning.

By most readers the Franconia stories are counted the

liveliest and most engaging of the Abbott books. Any child reading them today will receive a vivid impression of the pleasures of blueberrying and sleigh riding; he will learn about woodcutting and bear hunts; he will travel over mountain roads or sit before an open fire and roast apples on a string. Mostly vanished joys, to be sure, yet their very strangeness holds a kind of fascination.

With the Rainbow and Lucky series still another sober and industrious lad of fourteen is introduced to the reader. Rainbow is a colored boy whose methods of dealing with others are similar to those of Jonas and Beechnut, and so of their creator, Mr. Abbott. Lucky is a horse with an adequate amount of sense. Where did all the large assortment of curious names originate? In the account of Rainbow's journey on the ill-fated mountain stage alone, we meet Handie and Triggett, Jex and Hitover and Tolie; only the girls are called by such common names as Ruth and Melinda and Ann.

During the years from 1832 to 1879, this father of the story series, as he may properly be called, brought out fully two hundred books for young people, few of which reached the popularity of his major series. His method did not demand that he choose only short and easy words or write down to children's understanding. Instead, he used the words best suited to express his meaning, regardless of length, trusting that the young reader would ask his mother if he did not get the sense.

Together with his brother, John S. C. Abbott, author of a long biography of Napoleon, Jacob produced the little red histories, fondly regarded for many years. Through them even older people became aware of famous kings and queens who played important parts in the life of great nations. Among others, Abraham Lincoln made warm acknowledgment of the debt he owed these books.

If the vein seems all but exhausted in the thin quarto volumes appearing as Harper's Story Books, each month for several years, an occasional gleam here and there rewards the seeker, as in *Timboo and Joliba; or, The Art of Being Useful.* Timboo was an olive-skinned boy, born of a savage mother on an island in the South Seas. We are not informed by what strange circumstance he becomes a sailor and arrives in New York, bringing his parrot, Joliba, with him. Faint copy of Beechnut, as he is, he immediately begins to be useful, sleeping in a hogshead and doing chores for the Cheveril family, but his best good deed, after teaching himself to read, was the instruction of Fanny Cheveril, aged five. Fanny did not like to go to school because she had nothing to do there, except sit still on a bench until it was her turn to go forward to the teacher to read. In Timboo's opinion, "The two reasons why children are sent to school are, first, that they may learn to read and write, and secondly, to get rid of their noise and the trouble they make at home." Just for the light it throws upon the school situation, this is an instructive story.

Education, indeed, was the supreme interest of the author. All his ideas on the subject were forward-looking, growing out of his deep respect for children as individuals. Both in the home and in the school, Jacob Abbott worked for a closer understanding, and an equalizing relationship between the teacher and the taught. One of the innovations when he was principal of the Mount Vernon School for Girls, in Boston, was the introduction of self-government and the honor system. In a day when corporal punishment was the rule in schools and in families, Mr. Abbott's *Gentle Measures in the Management and Training of the Young* did much to bring about a more wholesome attitude in the upbringing of children.

With his own children he was quick to commend, and firm when it was necessary to control them. Sharing intimately the lives of his motherless boys, he, with an inborn sympathy, gained an insight into child nature in general. What country boy could fail to appreciate and enjoy the significance of this advice in the "Code Barbarian," sent by Jacob Abbott from New York, in a newspaper letter to his boys in Maine:

"When you come in from sliding leave your sled in the yard upon the snow.

It will rust the irons a little and may prevent its going too fast when you go out to slide next time. You may save breaking your neck by this means.

If you lose your knife or anything it is a convenient plan to tell some boy that you lent it to him one day and you have not seen it since."

Possibly, in spite of the remoteness of the leisurely days when there was time to teach children to handle tools and do chores, there are still elements in the best of the Abbott books that are worth the consideration of those who have to do with boys and girls.

SUSAN WARNER AND HER "WIDE, WIDE WORLD"

VI

TWO years after its publication in 1850 in two plump volumes, *The Wide, Wide World*, that famous story so dear to Mid-Victorian girlhood both in England and America, had reached its thirteenth edition. The charm has not yet wholly vanished from the recital of Ellen Montgomery's sorrows. Those who, reading widely among the letters and biographies of our grandmothers, chance upon more than one allusion to young ladies who sat in cold rooms and wept over *The Wide, Wide World*, may justly wonder where the charm lay. Perhaps only by reading this old-fashioned, sentimental story can we arrive at the answer, for which few in these crowded days, overfull of shorter books, have patience to search.

Just as Peter Parley introduced the authentic American scene into children's books and Jacob Abbott peopled it with real children, so Susan Warner seems to have been the first writer to combine for girls in their teens American characters with the national background.

As we look back to the other books written for girls during the first half of the nineteenth century we are obliged to turn again to England to find any that have left a mark. Susan Warner read the books of Mrs. Sherwood and Maria Edgeworth in her childhood and Miss Edgeworth's little girls must have been her only models worthy the name. There is, in the visit to the New York shops taken by Ellen Montgomery before parting with her mother, a faint echo of Rosamond's well-known shopping expedition when she bought the purple jar. But with a difference. It is for a Bible, one not too large, nor yet with too fine print, that Ellen is seeking. A strongly religious note pervades every production of the author of *The Wide, Wide World*.

The Warner sisters grew up in the atmosphere of books, with a father who read Boswell's *Life of Johnson* aloud to his daughters and awaited with them each new novel by Scott as it was issued. Susan was born in 1819 and lived all her life among the scenes she has chosen to draw under the pen name of Elizabeth Wetherell.

The Wide, Wide World was her first book, begun at the suggestion of an aunt and named by Anna Warner, her adoring younger sister. Written mainly at Constitution Island, three hundred yards off West Point in the Hudson River, and read to the family for approval, the book was not quick to find a publisher. Mr. Warner himself undertook to market it and one disappointment followed another until it came into the hands of George P. Putnam, who gave it serious consideration. Mr. Putnam, in grave doubt as to its availability, turned the manuscript over to his mother to read and from her came the verdict: "If you never publish another book you should publish this." Later events proved the soundness of her judgment, as *The Wide, Wide World* became immediately popular. It was reprinted many times, large numbers were sold in England and it was translated into several other languages.

Perhaps it may not be far wrong to call this story the first important example of the Sunday-school book type. Characteristic of the group is an atmosphere of fervent evangelism, overlaid with sentimentality, both religious and secular. As time went on such books took on a tone of self-righteousness in addition to their other qualities, and became altogether very distasteful to many sincere persons of the orthodox faith. "Too emotional for children," a London review of 1853 pronounced Susan Warner's famous book. Yet the *Edinburgh Witness* asserted that the author "has few equals and no superiors on either side of the Atlantic," and the *New York Times* stoutly declared that "one book like this is not produced in an age."

A state of copious tearfulness is inseparably connected with *The Wide, Wide World* in the memory of many readers. And no wonder. A few of the different phrases used to express Ellen's grief may be selected at random, yielding these expressions of sorrow:

"Ellen sat down and began to cry." (Ellen) "burst into tears." (Ellen) "threw herself on the floor in an agony of grief"; "quivering from head to foot with convulsive sobs"; "burst into one of those uncontrollable agonies of weeping"; "tears of mingled sweet and bitter were poured out fast"; "hiding her face in her hands"; "tears wet upon her cheek"; "tears fell like rain."

The theme is a favorite one. In Ellen Montgomery we have youth and innocence subjected to the hard knocks by which a callous world is apt to buffet children deprived of the natural protection of their parents and more or less at the mercy of the indifferent. Aunt Fortune was a singularly hardhearted guardian, especially in the matter of appropriating Ellen's letters without letting her see them. She is vividly described in the book.

In spite of her ready tears, however, the little girl has real personality and her grief over separation from her beloved mother, her longing for letters and her pathetic loneliness in the crude farming community touched the hearts of young and old. Her childish confidence was constantly winning friends. Among others there was the old gentleman who helped her buy a merino dress before leaving New York, who made her a present of a good warm winter hood and a brace of woodcock; there was the gentleman on the Hudson River boat who talked to her about the comforts of religion;

there was Mr. Van Brunt, the friendly Dutch farmer; there were Alice and John Humphreys, and Nancy, the naughty girl. One of the best portraits in the book is that of the jovial Mr. Van Brunt. Ellen's arrival at her aunt's home in his oxcart makes a delightful picture of a way of travel, strange enough to readers of the present day.

A strange, new world Ellen found it on Aunt Fortune's farm. Life there was more rigorous than that of her own home. When Ellen rose in the morning, the following day, she was bidden to go to bathe at a wooden tub fed by water flowing in wooden troughs from the spring; her white stockings splashed in the mud of the marsh were promptly dyed slate color; city ways must be laid aside.

Except for short glimpses of New York the setting of *The Wide, Wide World* and of *Queechy*, Miss Warner's very successful second book, is the home of her grandfather, just west of the Massachusetts border. Both books are undoubtedly based on many of the experiences of her own girlhood. Certainly the difficult adjustments between conditions of affluence and of poverty, described in both books, are the result of a kindred situation in the circumstances of the Warner family. Like the household in *Queechy*, Susan knew what it was to give up the amenities of the city and adapt herself to a society that seemed rude and restricted. The old news carrier with snuff-colored coat, broad-brimmed hat and tin trumpet was to her an arresting figure, as expressive of the countryside as the bees for pork chopping, corn husking and apple paring or the donation party for the new minister, all of which she describes with zest and humor.

Her love for the woods and fields of Canaan, for its farmlands, its old houses, the sawmill and the stream that turned it and for Queechy Lake itself is apparent on many pages. All the outdoor world with its infinite variety of sunset and moonlight, snowstorms and sunny days was a source of joy and inspiration which she could not keep out of her books.

A larger stage is set for the characters in *Queechy* than for those in *The Wide, Wide World;* indeed, it might be called a novel were it not that to the Warner sisters the name connoted something worldly and dangerous. Their point of view is reflected in the promise not to read novels, exacted from Ellen Montgomery by Mr. John, when that insufferable prig and pedant leaves her in Scotland with her fine relations. Fleda, the heroine of *Queechy*, is an orphan who early in the book loses her closest of kin, the grandfather in whom her whole world centers. Though less tearful than Ellen, she shows her delicate sensibilities by the inevitable headache following any strain upon her emotions. She is a child of sunshine, however, swift to see the right thing, wise to meet every emergency, considerate and self-sacrificing, constant in her Christian faith. But these qualities are not enough. Her ideals of what is true and beautiful in character and in nature are matched not only by her happy and cheerful temperament, but equally by her unfailing competence in practical affairs. We meet her at eleven years old as her watchful eyes are traveling disapprovingly over the old mare's rope-bound harness with a determination to have it adequately repaired. Whenever provisions ran a little short it was Fleda, even at this age, who could toss up a delicious omelette. Until her twentieth year, when the book leaves her, she never falters in doing the right thing, never fails to win the approbation of old and young for her matchless loveliness and simplicity.

With her wide acquaintance among the West Point cadets it is singular that the young men in Miss Warner's books are so stilted and unreal. Far more natural and lifelike are many of those who have minor parts. While the author states that only the cat in *The Wide, Wide World* is a portrait, we can hardly believe that she had not met with the originals of the independent "hired help," of whom Barby is an admirable example, else she could not have written of them with such sympathy and discernment.

But it is in the naïve and illuminating pictures of society in New York and the surrounding country nearly one hundred years ago that readers of *Queechy* may still find entertainment. This was the New York of Dickens' *American Notes*, where finery was flaunted on the streets on which barefoot little girls swept the crossings and ragged boys sold matches, where the street cries of oystermen and chimney sweeps could still be heard. Fleda and her friends dress in fine embroidered muslins for evening levees in elegant drawing rooms to engage in earnest conversations with young men about the true sphere of woman, or to display their skill in worsted work before admiring eyes. Fleda herself is distinctly bookish in her tastes, even contributing essays and poems to newspapers and magazines. When she is in town visiting her great-uncle, the library is a favorite haunt. She shows herself able to quote from Shakespeare and Burke, or to repeat Bryant's poems if occasion requires; but to her, the Bible is the most precious book.

During the years the Warners lived on Constitution Island Susan was actively employed in writing, though none of her later stories attained the popularity of the two earliest. Taking a series name from her most admired heroine she brought out *Ellen Montgomery's Book Shelf*, which had formerly a certain vogue, especially in Sunday-school libraries. One of these books, intended for quite young children, deserves not to be wholly forgotten because of its engaging picture of a pair of happy little sisters in town and country life. As *Mr. Rutherford's Children* is attributed to "The Authors of *The Wide, Wide World*," it seems certain that Anna had a share in its writing. The two children, Sybil and Chryssa, are seen in a normal setting with affectionate and understanding elders, enjoying a protected, wholesome childhood. From their winter stay at a famous hotel in New York, we get an agreeable picture of the way in which well-to-do families in the great city educated and diverted their children in the middle years of the last century.

It was unquestionably rare at that time for an American writer of children's books to have so genuine a background of both city and country environment. The Warners had moved in generous and cultivated circles in New York before the loss of their property made it necessary to retrench by retiring to the country. On the other hand, even in the days of prosperity, their summers were spent among simple folk where it was but natural that an appreciative observer, like Miss Susan, should note contrasts and differences peculiar to rural surroundings. And since, in 1840, more than one-fourth of the people of the United States were engaged in agriculture, the great popularity of her stories may be the better understood.

As their years advanced it is pleasant to think of the old Revolutionary house on Constitution Island where Miss Susan and Miss Anna dwelt for many years, the older sister until her death in 1885, the younger living until 1915 and with her other occupations there writing a life of her sister Susan. Both were buried with military honors in the Government cemetery at West Point. The West Point boys found in the house on the island a welcome escape from the restraints of Academy limits, for the ladies were kind and hospitable. Their friendship was of a lasting quality, and followed the young soldiers into the world with years of faithful correspondence.

One of the cadets has left a becoming portrait of Susan Warner as she sat in a big chair in the orchard on Sunday afternoons surrounded by boys on the grass, while she talked on some religious subject, earnestly and with no cant or sectarianism. After her talk came the treat to which they had looked forward for a week, tea and homemade gingerbread. "She looked," he said, "like a print from *Godey's Lady's Book*. She always wore silk dresses of a small flowered pattern made with voluminous skirts of wonderful stiffness and rustle, and small, close-fitting bodices. A rich Paisley shawl was always around her shoulders, and a broad black velvet ribbon was bound around her hair."

So she should, indubitably, have looked and we may leave Miss Susan, confident for once that the actor fits the part.

THE DAWN OF IMAGINATION
IN AMERICAN BOOKS FOR
CHILDREN

VII

LOOK in any authoritative reading list for children and you will find *A Wonder-Book* and *Tanglewood Tales* holding high place among retellings from the Greek myths. They have been named in such lists for many years now, kept alive by children's deep affection, always coming freshly to a new generation, to whom they are as dear as they were to Caroline Hewins, a child of the mid-century, who found *A Wonder-Book* on her pillow when she opened her eyes on the morning of her seventh birthday. "The dear green *Wonder-Book* with the Hammatt Billings pictures of the group of children on Tanglewood porch."

Not far from one hundred years ago, while American children's books were still cast in the matter-of-fact world set by Peter Parley and Jacob Abbott, Hawthorne wrote to his publisher, from his home in Lenox, announcing his intention of writing, within the next six weeks, a book of stories from Greek mythology, to which he proposed to give a romantic rather than a classical turn. That was in May, 1851. *A Wonder-Book* was finished and the Preface written on the fifteenth of July of that year. In presenting these myths to children, Hawthorne allowed his imagination to range over the bare elements of the immortal stories and clothe them in warm, intimate details that appeal to a child's mind. He was at no pains to keep their classical aspect; on the contrary, he deliberately shed it, believing that to embroider these myths with his own idealistic fancy was legitimate, in no way affecting their essential spirit. So, Hawthorne thought, the ancient poets themselves had dealt with the stories handed down from a still earlier world. He anticipated the critics who have not approved of this freedom, making his defense in the Prefaces to the books, where he claims that the old legends cannot be injured by certain changes in form, as they are the common property of mankind.

The two books together retell, in modern language, a dozen of the great stories from classic authors—six in each volume. In *A Wonder-Book* the thread of framing story is an integral part of the book with the student storyteller, surrounded by his circle of story lovers, responsible for the rendering of each myth. This first collection of Greek myths seems, indeed, a wonder book, so different is it in playful fancy and charm of style from all other books written for children in the first half of the nineteenth century. Hawthorne's earlier work for children had included his contributions to Peter Parley's publications, often innocent and ethereal, and the childlike narratives of early New England history, contained in *Grandfather's Chair* and *Biographical Stories*, published by Elizabeth Peabody, sister of Sophia, Hawthorne's wife. They show his romantic nature and his sympathy with children and foreshadow his Greek fairy tales.

Greek mythology, far from being a remote choice of subject for a child's book in the mid-nineteenth century, was a natural world for Hawthorne's imagination to roam when he decided to allow himself a pleasant relaxation from more strenuous literary tasks. Massachusetts had been strongly influenced by the Greek revival, following the close of the War of 1812, strengthened there by the ardor of local scholars and hero-worshippers. Books, lectures and classic sculpture united to focus attention upon Greek literature and mythology, and the Hawthorne children were not the only ones to feel the irresistible fascination of the old stories. Only, with them, the association was closer because the household possessed many copies of John Flaxman's graceful designs drawn for his outlines of the *Iliad* and the *Odyssey*, and carefully traced by Mrs. Hawthorne who loved them.

One questions whether there is any other author whose books for children show a greater contrast to those intended for adult readers. If we compare *The Scarlet Letter*, the novel just completed, from which Hawthorne took flight to a lighter mood, with the Greek fairy tales, the difference is marked, indeed. The fresh, sunny atmosphere of *A Wonder-Book* gives added weight to his family's belief that he was at his happiest in these months at Lenox. He had left his irksome post at the Salem Custom House and had finished his work on his greatest novel. Now he was a new man, giving himself to his children, sharing with them their games and pleasures, accompanying them on walks and climbs among the beautiful Berkshire hills. With them he was a gay and playful comrade, far other than the man so often termed gloomy by his contemporaries.

Tanglewood, where the Hawthornes lived for rather less than two years, was a red story-and-a-half farmhouse on the lonely road from Stockbridge to Lenox, in the heart of the Berkshires. When Hawthorne walked with his children in the woods and across the fields, delighting in the beauty of the landscape, sensitive to the changing seasons, he rejoiced in his freedom. Amidst these surroundings the narrative binding together the Greek fairy tales has its setting.

The Introductions to the stories are all tuned to the special place where each story was supposed to be told, with the color and feeling of country days from autumn to late spring. The warmth and haze of an Indian summer morning hover over the telling of "The Gorgon's Head," when the children, with their flower names, were gathered around Eustace Bright on the porch at Tanglewood. At noon, the party were eating their lunch in a dell at Shadow Brook after a forenoon's fun in nutting, and here they listened to the young student's version of "The Golden Touch." Just before Christmas, as a heavy snow was falling, the college boy, home for the holidays, kept the Tanglewood children absorbed in the playroom over Pandora's troubles, while the next day, in "a magnificent palace of snow," he told about the "Three Golden Apples." It was in Maytime that the series was finished on the hilltop, with "The Miraculous Pitcher" and "The Chimaera."

Some of Hawthorne's most delightful descriptive writing is to be found in these Introductions. His eyes, always responsive to beauty, noted how the morning mists filled the valley and hid the tops of the encircling mountains, how the bright yellow leaves sprinkled golden sunshine over the brook, how the fluttering snowflakes mantled the trees and frozen lake in dazzling white. He knew the little brook in all its aspects, rushing merrily along over the stones or tinkling under its icy banks of snow. His, too, was the sure knowledge of a New England spring with its cherished wild flowers breaking the cold ground—arbutus and violets, columbine and "that sociablest of flowers, the little Houstonia," for which he evidently felt a special affection.

As the children climbed the hillside in the spring and looked far to the west, they saw a range of blue mountains which, Eustace Bright told them, were the Catskills. "Among those misty hills, he said, was a spot where some

old Dutchmen were playing an everlasting game of nine-
pins, and where an idle fellow, whose name was Rip Van
Winkle, had fallen asleep, and slept twenty years at a
stretch." When the children begged for that story, Eustace
replied that the story "had been told once already, and better
than it ever could be told again; and that nobody would
have a right to alter a word of it until it should have grown
as old as 'The Gorgon's Head,' and 'The Three Golden
Apples,' and the rest of those miraculous legends."

Tanglewood Tales were written at Wayside, in Concord.
Hawthorne mentioned the date of their completion, March
9, 1853, in his *American Notebooks*, together with the order
of their writing: "The Pomegranate Seeds," "The Minotaur,"
"The Golden Fleece," "The Dragon's Teeth," "Circe's
Palace," "The Pygmies." This is not the arrangement in the
published book, as it now appears. To these later tales there
is but one Introduction, when Eustace Bright, now a college
senior, turns over to the editor his "wild stories from the
classic myths," which in his own estimation were better
chosen and better handled than those of *A Wonder-Book*.
Whether or not this is true, countless numbers of English-
reading children have been grateful these many years that
Hawthorne opened for them the gateway to Greek mythology through these matchless stories.

Less than a generation ago, children in New England still
read with pleasure *The Last of the Huggermuggers* and *Kobboltozo*, two fanciful tales written a year or two after *Tangle-*

wood Tales appeared. Unlike Hawthorne's stories, they derived nothing from the Greek classics, but perhaps it may be thought that the author's imagination drew a little upon *Gulliver's Travels*. When the two stories, written in Paris by Christopher P. Cranch, in 1855-1856, were sent to friends in Boston for publication, they were counted a decided success.

Both books have to do with the fabulous experiences of a young sailor, Jacket or Jacky, who was shipwrecked in the East Indies, not far from Java. On the island where he and a few companions were cast up, everything was of enormous size, for here lived two giants, the Huggermuggers, last of their race. Little Jacket, sleeping in a huge sea shell, was picked up by one of the giants, who desired the shell as a present for his wife, without seeing its unusual occupant. Thenceforward, the story flows on over Jacket's adventures with the giants, who proved to be a good and kindly pair, lonely in their large house because they had no companions except a race of dwarfs, and glad to make friends with the castaways. An exploring trip afforded many strange sights on the island and brought acquaintance with the colony of dwarfs, with which the second book, *Kobboltozo*, is concerned. *The Last of the Huggermuggers* ends too sadly for children, as Mrs. Huggermugger dies and her lonely mate, taken off the island by Jacket in a Yankee ship, does not survive the voyage to America.

Kobboltozo is an account of a second visit to the island,

when Jacky learns what happened there after he and the giants had gone. There was one malicious dwarf, named Kobboltozo, whose jealous nature had actually caused the end of the race of giants. He and his companions were eager to grow big and inherit the island and Kobboltozo had succeeded in learning a part of the secret of becoming great. This lay in eating a magic shellfish to be found on the shore. Since no one knew which was the right shellfish among the different varieties, the dwarfs spent their time sampling many kinds, with the result that most of them became smaller and vanished away. Kobboltozo was found by Jacket in a cave, still eating oysters and no larger than he ever was.

This is a livelier story than *The Last of the Huggermuggers*. It has more humor and some delightful descriptions of the wonderful caves where gnomes tended their forges, where lived the witch and the Mer-king. Illustrated by Mr. Cranch with pencil drawings, similar to those of Thackeray, there is not a little charm in the allegory, possibly better appreciated by adults than by children. It was the Mer-king who sang an interpretive song.

> "Not in the Ocean deep and clear,
>   Not on the Land so broad and fair,
>   Not in the regions of boundless Air,
>   Not in the Fire's burning sphere—
>   'Tis not here—'tis not there.

Ye may seek it everywhere.
He that is a dwarf in spirit
Never shall the isle inherit.
Hearts that grow 'mid daily cares
Grow to greatness unawares;
Noble souls alone may know
How the giants live and grow."

Christopher Pearse Cranch was a versatile and gifted American who shared with Hawthorne some of the ideals of the transcendentalists, like him finding congenial friends in the community at Brook Farm, in the 1840's. Handsome and graceful, with an agreeable singing voice and easy facility at the piano and with the flute, Cranch was always a welcome guest. He had an eye for caricature, too, and did not hesitate to make fun in his cartoons of such a dignified friend as Emerson, though with the utmost good nature. Too variously gifted, possibly too indolent, to become distinguished in any field, Christopher Cranch wrote several volumes of poetry and painted many pictures, but little of his work in either field has lasted. Years of travel and residence abroad in Italy, France and England brought him in touch with the Brownings and Thackeray and their circles. His own four children liked the giant and dwarf stories, but wept over the end of the Huggermuggers.

Cranch's friends urged him to continue writing books for children, for they felt he could improve upon what he had done. W. W. Story, the sculptor, begged him to put his energies into his writing and lighten it with more fun and gaiety. "If you can," he writes, "let it hold a double story, an internal one and an external one, as Andersen's do, so that the wiseacres shall like it as well as the children. Read 'The Little Tin Soldier,' 'The Ugly Duckling' and 'The Emperor's New Clothes.' You *can* do this and you *must*." James Russell Lowell and George William Curtis bestowed their approval upon his rare faculty of invention, but neither was wholly satisfied with their friend's achievement. For, in spite of his poet's feeling and artist's eye, all this good advice could not make a Hans Christian Andersen out of Christopher Cranch.

ELIJAH KELLOGG AND THE ELM ISLAND BOYS

VIII

SIX miles off the Maine coast "broad off at sea" lay Elm Island, home of Lion Ben and Charlie Bell, cradle of the "Ark" and the "Hardscrabble," mecca for the Young Ship Builders and Boy Farmers. Heavily wooded with spruce, interspersed with fir and hemlock, at one end there was a grove of elm trees which gave the small island its name. There were maples enough to form a good sugar bush and a famous beech tree in which the herons nested. From the rockbound shores high cliffs rose up at intervals and one ran down to a quiet cove, safe harbor for boats, with a spring-nourished brook where frostfish and smelts came in, where wild geese, brant, sea ducks and other game birds settled in the fresh water.

Here, and on the neighboring mainland, the enterprises described in the Elm Island and Pleasant Cove series took place, those names beloved by hundreds of boys in the last quarter of the nineteenth century. The action of the stories and the attendant living conditions date back to the years just after the Revolutionary War, before the great days of shipbuilding in Maine, when the people on the coast were mostly pioneers, fishermen, farmers and small boatbuilders.

Lion Ben of Elm Island was the first book in the series. Young Ben Rhines, who gave up a sailor's life on the urgent plea of the girl he was to marry, is the central figure of the Elm Island stories. He had nothing but his hands and his narrow ax when he started to make a home for his Sally, whom he brought to the island in a squall of wind to the log cabin he had built in the woods. He hoped to pay for the island, which he had bought on credit, by cutting and selling masts and spars and other valuable lumber.

Stalwart is the fitting word for Lion Ben. A giant in stature with strength to match, it was nothing for him to pick up a canoe and "heave" it on shore like a bundle of chips, while with equal ease he could toss over his head any bully or braggart who crossed his path. With all his strength and hardihood this young man could be kind and gentle and his integrity was above reproach. Indeed, Ben and Sally "resembled in solidity the granite of their native soil." The younger boys to whom Ben was a hero, who looked to him for leadership, were his young relatives and the sons of the neighbors.

Industry and hard work tamed the wilderness for them,

ingenuity and energy turned every natural resource to good account. Fish from the sea and abundant wild fowl at their door provided the main food staples, supplemented in time by the produce from their garden. Turnips were the first vegetable crop planted.

Little by little the home place grew. Equipment needed for carrying on was fashioned mostly by hand labor. The loom that Sally wanted for weaving her homespun was made by Charlie Bell, the capable waif who blew in from Halifax and was adopted by Ben and Sally. The feathers for her pillows she plucked from the wild geese brought down by Ben's sure aim. Sally's carefully tended garden held the fragrant herbs she had brought from her mother's home, used as remedies in old New England, tansy, coltsfoot, wormwood, saffron, lovage and peppermint.

Since his tall trees held the best promise of advancing his fortunes, Lion Ben seems to have had an unusually intelligent grasp of the principles of conservation in contrast to methods followed by more grasping settlers. For Ben loved his island and did not want to strip it, "diminishing the fertility of the soil, exposing it to tempests, drying up the springs and defacing its beauty," so he cut economically and cleared only so much of the island as was needed for tillage.

Hewing spars from the straightest of his trees, Lion Ben bound them together and rafted them along the Maine coast on a voyage which ended at Long Wharf in Boston, where he netted enough to pay half the initial debt for his island.

Encouraged by this success, the ingenious settler planned a more daring project which is the subject of *The Ark of Elm Island*. In order to market his lumber without the aid of middlemen, he built a remarkable craft for a longer voyage. She was constructed of logs, made buoyant by casks, protected by the partial framework of a vessel and rigged as a fore-and-aft schooner. With a whimsical touch which is but seldom apparent in the chronicles of Elm Island, this curious vessel was named the "Ark," because, like Noah's boat of old, she carried a mixed cargo.

Captained by Ben's father, the "Ark" was manned by neighbors' boys and sailed to Cuba, where she was broken up and sold profitably. With the proceeds of the sale a brig was bought, loaded with molasses, coffee and sugar, and brought back to Boston.

Molasses was a desirable import in those days and it was by no means all turned into New England rum. Always desirable for cooking, it was sometimes the only sweetener to be found to satisfy the taste of the heavy toilers of the sea and shore. Every fishing boat carried twelve gallons of "long sweetening." No lumber camp would be without it.

The account of the "Ark's" arrival in Boston afforded an opportunity to set forth to rural readers the impression made on country boys by the sights of a large city, where one might even be invited to the home of a well-to-do merchant with whom the Captain could do business selling the cargo and even the brig herself. And the boys had money in their pockets, too, with which to pay for presents for the womenfolk at home, a shawl perhaps, or even a brooch. For the "Ark" not only took herself to market, but carried, as well, ventures by the crew including livestock, pigs and hens. It was in the handling of this mixed cargo in an uneasy sea that some of the dangers and accidents occurred which provided excitement and suspense on the voyage.

Absorbing as these details of pioneer industry are, the boys who loved the stories probably enjoyed as much some of the commoner episodes, like the country wrestling matches in which one can be sure Lion Ben will come out on top, though the struggle may be stiff. Or, perhaps, they liked better the thrilling fight in earnest with the piratical crew who brought Charlie Bell to the island, or maybe the hunting yarns of Uncle Isaac who could, and did, outrun more than one bull moose in the Maine woods.

Enough authentic matter is contained in *The Fisher Boys of Pleasant Cove* for it to be counted an historical picture of the fishing business of the Maine coast in the eighteenth and early nineteenth centuries. This unvarnished tale of the risks and hazards endured by Andrew Colcord recounts the experiences that were likely to befall men while "going over the Bay," to Fundy or Chaleur, to fish within a short distance of shore, sometimes in the track of ships inward or outward bound.

Boys who read the story learned that "going over the Bay" signified the practice of fishing near enough shore to come quickly into harbor with the catch, as distinguished from the practice followed by fishermen who made longer trips, salted their fish, and did not come home until they had used all their salt and "made their fare." They learned also, from this book, about the various fishing banks, about owners and outfitters and the rules for sharing the catch.

Each of the six books in the Elm Island series has a central theme of character-building import. *The Boy Farmers of Elm Island* stresses the importance of being ready to lend your neighbors a hand whenever there is need, as there so often was need in the sparsely settled regions where these pioneers dwelt.

One truth is implicit in all these stories, that character develops rapidly under pressure and the spur of necessity. No hint of an expectation of easy success or quickly gained riches enters into any of Kellogg's books. Endurance, self-sacrifice, pluck and upright living, the dignity of work, the worth of a plain man are emphasized in all his stories, told in the Maine vernacular and with a thoroughgoing knowledge of fishing, farming and boatbuilding. If the characters do not always come to life, if their conversations are frequently stiff and unnatural, their adventures have the ring of truthfulness.

Three series of Kellogg's books, six volumes in each, are to be found in *Books for the Young* by Caroline Hewins.

Besides Elm Island stories and the Pleasant Cove series, she listed the Forest Glen series among the books on North American travel and adventure. The Forest Glen series, of which the best known book is *Wolf Run*, is laid in a frontier settlement in western Pennsylvania, not far from Braddock's old battlefield. The books are mainly concerned with Indian warfare over the disputed territory claimed alike by the province of Pennsylvania and the Indians of the locality, Mohawks and Delawares.

The first, and by all odds the best, though not the most popular of Elijah Kellogg's books, is *Good Old Times; or Grandfather's Struggles for a Homestead*. Announced in the prospectus of *Our Young Folks*, for 1867, as the leading story of the year, it gives a vivid picture of American customs and manners a century earlier. From the frontier experiences of his own great-grandfather, Hugh McLellan, among the first settlers in Gorham, Kellogg drew the material for a detailed story of life in Maine before the Revolution, when conditions were primitive and toilsome.

Early settlers then found their most lucrative employment in mast hauling. Regal pines towered in the forests. Every sound straight tree over thirty-six inches in diameter was marked by the broad arrow of the king, to be felled and taken to the coast by ox teams.

Good Old Times holds the fascination of other books which show how Americans managed in pioneer settlements before the industrial age, when eight-foot sticks blazed on a farmer's hearth of an evening, with a dish of apples temptingly standing between the andirons. Such inviting details as the pleasures of picking blueberries in abundance and gathering beechnuts and acorns make the times seem good, indeed, but the grimmer side comes to light with the description of the old blockhouse at Gorham and the garrisons against Indian raids.

Widely known and widely loved in New England, Elijah Kellogg, the man who wrote these books, was well qualified to speak with authority about farmers, fishermen and sailors, for he had not only lived among them, but had also tried a hand at all three occupations. In his boyhood customs had not changed greatly from those described in the Elm Island and Pleasant Cove books.

There were two Elijah Kelloggs. The father had been a drummer boy with the minutemen in 1775, had fought at Bunker Hill and Ticonderoga and had shared the privations of Valley Forge. After the Revolutionary War he went to Dartmouth College, became a minister and preached many years in Portland. He was greatly beloved and greatly influential along the Maine coast, especially in his missionary days when he had finished his settled pastorate and journeyed to the eastward speaking to the people along the way. Parson Kellogg had, by inheritance, a freedom-loving spirit and an uncompromising Puritanism.

Young Elijah, born in 1813, drew a similar inheritance of sturdy independence from his mother also, granddaughter of the Gorham pioneer, Hugh McLellan. The small city of Portland was too narrow for the boy's activities and he ran away to sea at thirteen, to spend three years before the mast in Maine sailing vessels. After the urge for roving wore itself off, Elijah came ashore for a turn at farming and it was then that he realized that he needed an education. This meant preparation at the famous old Academy at Gorham, and earning the money for entering Bowdoin College, from which he graduated in 1840, going from there to Andover to study for the ministry.

Cruising around Casco Bay while he was still a college student, Kellogg discovered the long narrow neck of land which, with forty near-by islands, comprised the parish of Harpswell. The boy, whom the sea had called very early, fell under the spell of the seagirt village, returning there for every possible vacation and identifying himself with the kind of life that went on there. The shipbuilders, fishermen and retired sailors who lived in the township liked this friendly young man as much as he liked them, and before Elijah had graduated from Bowdoin he had promised to return there as preacher. Trusting in his good faith, the men of Harpswell built for him a church where his memory is still fondly cherished as a graceful orator and a devoted pastor.

When he finished his theological training, Elijah Kellogg went back to Harpswell to become pastor of the church for a salary of three hundred dollars, and though interrupting his service to act as Chaplain of the Sailors' Home in Boston, he never severed his connection with Harpswell and its citizens.

His twenty-nine books, written in Boston, have on some of their title pages a note to the effect that he was the author of "Spartacus to the Gladiators," an identification that gave him great prestige in the days when rhetorical exercises were a part of all college programs. For this speech became a tested favorite for prize declamations and was seldom absent from collections of oratorical writing compiled for school contests. Dozens of boys have stood on platforms in assembly halls and mouthed the opening words, written and spoken by a young theological student:

"Ye call me chief, and ye do well to call him chief who, for twelve long years, has met upon the arena every shape of man or beast the broad empire of Rome could furnish, and who never yet has lowered his arm."

Now there is nothing apparent in the mere facts of Elijah Kellogg's life, nor in his books, that would account for the high esteem in which his name has been held at Bowdoin College and at other spots along the coast of Maine. The reason must be sought in the nature of the man himself. He was loved for his quick sympathies, his kindness and generosity, his fearlessness for the right, his otherworldliness.

All his life, too, Elijah Kellogg had a strong element of the mischief-loving boy with a keen sense of fun. He kept the ready wit which came to his aid in early years and caused him to lay the blame for his being late to school on the frogs, which had screamed K'logg K'logg, so insistently, that he felt obliged to turn back to see what they wanted.

Many stories are told of his personal courage, strength and self-reliance, the qualities he sought to arouse in his boys. Tradition gives the name of Elijah Kellogg as that of the first man to climb the spire of the college chapel to place the president's hat atop it. It was more than forty years before another daring Maine boy matched the reckless deed and put his class flag there.

The books that Kellogg wrote were prompted by a desire to help boys live upright lives. They never emphasize the making of money, though a practical regard for a decent living is not lacking. While he was at Harpswell it was a common practice for the college authorities to send him students who had to be "rusticated," to make up deficiencies in their academic work. They learned to study there and to revere his wise advice. Thus he became dear to thousands of boys and a college president was moved to write with all earnestness, "It will be a sad day for Bowdoin College if there shall ever be a generation of students who know not Elijah Kellogg."

HORACE E. SCUDDER,
CRITIC AND EDITOR

IX

I T is counted almost an axiom that a sound foundation of comparative values is essential for an intelligent approach to book selection for children. Best of all is to know good books at first hand, by reading them in childhood, thus carving a scale for measuring the ever-growing mass of current publications. For those are the precious reading years when one learns to know the difference between a real hero and a sham superman. Was Matthew Arnold right in his famous dictum that criticism is "a disinterested endeavor to learn and propagate the best that is known and thought in the world," and does this rule apply to those who discuss children's books? There were those who thought so in the nineteenth century, before there were children's librarians or children's book editors in publishing houses.

In the twenty-five years from 1870-1895 the two dominating influences affecting for good the production of children's literature in America were the *St. Nicholas* magazine, under the editorship of Mary Mapes Dodge in New York, and the editorial work of Horace E. Scudder in Boston. Believing that books for children should be judged by the same standards of criticism that govern the consideration of general literature, both Mrs. Dodge and Mr. Scudder made certain demands upon their contributors. Each had tireless energy and finely balanced judgment. So they set themselves to the task of providing boys and girls with reading that was worthy of their intelligence in the hope that young people would thus learn to distinguish the good from the bad for themselves.

Horace E. Scudder was a New Englander, the youngest son in a family of seven children, boys all but one. He was generously endowed with a strong sense of spiritual values, a love of music and art, and a discerning literary taste. During his years at college the Greek poets were his great delight and all through life he read from the Greek Testament every day. When he graduated from Williams College at twenty years of age he held the determination to pursue a literary career of some kind, though as yet he did not see his course plainly. His first published work grew out of his friendship for children. A little handful of fanciful stories written in that exquisite handwriting which he retained all his life, illustrated by himself and tied with ribbons, remains as witness of the pains he took to give enjoyment to his younger friends. These early stories show the tender sympathy Mr. Scudder always had with child life. They are permeated by a spirit of kinship with the imaginary world so real to children and to those older persons who have been blessed with an inborn gift of mysticism.

There was little sound criticism of children's books in the late sixties, so when Mr. Scudder introduced a series of articles on "Books for Young People" into a children's magazine which he had planned, it was a true innovation. *The Riverside Magazine*, whose brief existence of four years (1867-1870) was marked by this unusual feature, was his first venture as an editor. His editorials written to introduce the subject of children's reading and express his views on the parents' responsibility for making a right choice are full of meat. "What is it to a child," he asks, "whether a book was first published in hot haste this Christmas or has lain on the counters for a year, and is now, maybe, rather dull in cloth beside its new companions, though then it was thought brilliant enough? We may as well discard at once all such unnecessary considerations as when a book was published, or where it was published, and come right at the gist of the matter and ask if it is *good*,—good in itself and adapted to the reader for whom we are buying it."

And again, "We shall pay no very close attention to the line which divides books written for the young from books written for the old, but making a survey of literature, single out those writings which are worth giving to a child and for an acquaintance with which he will always hold us in grateful remembrance."

It was a delightful monthly, *The Riverside Magazine for Young People*. Think of looking forward to reading every month or so a new story by Hans Christian Andersen never before published! For several of these made their first appearance through the pages of *The Riverside Magazine*, and were later printed in Denmark. Altogether seventeen stories by Andersen came out in the *Riverside* in the course of its four years. There was much good poetry, too, ballads and famous verse as well as stories by some of the best writers of the day. But in the care bestowed upon the illustrations *The Riverside Magazine* struck a wholly new note for its time. To obtain pictures that he considered worthy of putting before children, Mr. Scudder searched far and wide. The measure of his success is indicated by the list of illustrations for 1867, which includes the names of John La Farge, Thomas Nast, Winslow Homer, E. B. Bensell, H. L. Stephens and F. O. C. Darley. "I did my best," said he in speaking of this feature, "to obtain pictures of child life from painters who were not mere professional book illustrators. It was only now and then that I was able to obtain any simple, unaffected design, showing an understanding of a child's figure and face." A few years after *The Riverside Magazine* ceased publication some of its valued contributors became closely connected with *St. Nicholas*, started by Mary

Mapes Dodge in 1873. Mr. Scudder was warmly interested in its development and was content to have it in his home for his daughter to read with her Andersen and Grimm, Mrs. Ewing and George Macdonald.

As a member of the house of Hurd and Houghton, the predecessors of the Houghton Mifflin Company, a connection established in 1872, Mr. Scudder had still greater opportunity to emphasize the importance of children's reading. About this time he was writing for the *New York Tribune:* "This distinction between books for children and books for their elders, so purely a creation of the last hundred years, ought to be abolished in our schools, and the better lesson taught of the common inheritance held by children with their parents in the great literature of the nation and parent country. If it is objected that this is impossible, that children cannot understand classic English literature, we reply—try them and see."

The idea of the "Riverside Literature Series for Young People" began to take shape in his mind. The impulse toward this series of whole works instead of fragments for the use of schools came from his dissatisfaction with the old-fashioned school readers. These, he felt, contained many scraps, sometimes from excellent sources but very seldom of the first quality. Mr. Scudder's theory was that anything in English and American literature which lives by virtue of its common acceptance may safely be made a part of the school curriculum. But he wanted reading to be a joy and not a task. The right kind of reading should be chosen "to stimulate interest, rouse the imagination and fix the attention, reading at the same time healthy and sound and which shall lead to better things in the future." In this series of worthwhile literature designed largely for use in schools the format and the low cost played important parts. Each regular number in paper covers cost but fifteen cents and was of a size to go easily into pockets for reading at leisure. Longfellow's "Evangeline" was the first poem selected for the series, a natural choice at that period. But later numbers went farther and put a great store of English as well as American classics within the reach of young people with slender resources. Unquestionably, the "Riverside Literature Series" has been a great influence in the forming of taste and appreciation in countless young people, in school and out.

What were the children's books published by the Houghton Mifflin Company during the years when Mr. Scudder was its literary adviser? Sarah Orne Jewett, who had written for *The Riverside Magazine*, brought them *Betty Leicester*. Eliza Orne White's first stories for children, *When Molly Was Six* and *A Little Girl of Long Ago*, belong to those years. There were books by Joel Chandler Harris and Mrs. A. D. T. Whitney, Whittier's lovely anthology, *Child Life*, and many others. Especially important were the two volumes of Hans Christian Andersen's work which Mr. Scudder regarded so highly that he studied Danish himself in order to be assured of the integrity of the translation. For years now these books have been considered the most complete and satisfactory, in point of text, published in this country.

Faithful adherence to the best version of a traditional work was his fixed principle. In this, Scudder sets an example for other editors of the old folk tales and fables. His splendid collection, *The Children's Book*, published in 1881, has never been equaled in comprehensiveness and authenticity. Miss Hewins said of it, "A child who has it for a companion knows the best that has been written in English for children." *The Children's Book* is, in truth, a triumph of editorial integrity and wisdom, as rewarding in a family of children now, if it can be obtained, as it was in the closing decades of the nineteenth century.

Without anywhere putting it into words, the editor arranged this treasury of good literature in a rising scale of difficulty, so a child may find his own level, unhampered by grade restrictions, if drawn to a particular story. A round dozen sections are spread over the large generous pages, starting with a considerable collection of easy fables from Aesop, since John Locke's day a classic for beginners. "The Book of Wonders," which comes next, contains favorite nursery tales, Chicken-Licken, the Three Bears, and Rumpelstilzchen among them, followed by Cinderella, Dick Whittington, Puss in Boots.

Four sections in different parts of the book present well-chosen poetry, lyrics, storytelling poems and ballads.

There is a representative selection of Andersen's tales under his name, so a child may identify the author with his work; another group brings together the best-liked stories from the *Arabian Nights;* elsewhere the most important parts of *A Voyage to Lilliput* and the *Travels of Baron Munchausen* widen familiarity with imaginative books. Mr. Scudder did not omit a few old-fashioned didactic stories with morals, like "Eyes and No Eyes," and *The Children's Book* ends with four great tales from the Greek.

With the exception of his life of Washington, still recognized as among the best of the one-volume lives of Washington, the creative work that Mr. Scudder intended for children has not lived. His volumes of fanciful stories, graceful in style and sympathetic though they are, make little appeal to the modern child. The doings of the active Bodley family have had their day of popularity and been superseded by other fashions in travel books. Yet, on fresh examination the eight volumes will be found to contain much information often amusingly imparted. They admit also ballads and legends and short stories from history which might even now be read to young children profitably. But perhaps Horace Scudder's original work is best represented for our purpose in the collection of addresses given as a Lowell Institute course in 1882 and published later under the title, *Childhood in Literature and Art*. This group of addresses dedicated to his daughter shows Mr. Scudder at his best. Because he loved his subject he wrote with enthusiasm and charm. They bear the marks of a scholar's wide research among classical writers and of an equally wide study of mediaeval art. To choose the changing aspects of child life as revealed in literature from Homer to Wordsworth for discussion in such a course of lectures is sufficient proof of the importance he placed upon it. Extensive reading and the thought of many years lie behind these essays. They are enriched by many allusions, many touching extracts, such as the tender passage in Homer where Hector takes leave of Andromache and little Astyanax. Following child life through these pages brings us in contact with famous works of art. Two chapters at the end of the book hold a special appeal. These are the chapter on Hans Christian Andersen and the one on "Childhood in American Literary Art." In the last there is much wise and discriminating comment upon Hawthorne's work and on later tendencies in children's books. But in his appreciation of Andersen's art Mr. Scudder greatly served his time. No one else in America has done so much to show the ingenuity and wit, the play of imagination, the form and grace of Andersen's delicate fairy tales. Even a factual minded person might be drawn to read Andersen by this glowing introduction.

As author and editor Mr. Scudder touched various fields and left a considerable number of works dealing with American history and biography as well as essays in keen literary criticism. But we cannot help feeling that he would wish to be remembered not so much for these or for his years as editor of *The Atlantic Monthly*, but rather, as he is, for his fundamental part in the establishment of a sane attitude toward children's books and reading.

"OUR YOUNG FOLKS": ITS EDITORS AND AUTHORS

X

FOR about ten years after the close of the Civil War boys and girls from reading families waited each month at post offices and country stores for the mail to bring them *Our Young Folks.* Launched from the same ways as *The Atlantic Monthly*, it sailed into many of the same homes where its elder sister was welcomed. First of the modern type of magazines for boys and girls, *Our Young Folks* made its appearance in gay orange paper covers with the names of its editors surrounding a well-clad Minerva complacently seated on the front. Dr. Oliver Wendell Holmes, who had named *The Atlantic Monthly*, wanted its young counterpart to be called *Atlantic Lighter*, but that may have seemed too flippant to the publishers, for the name chosen was more sedate and conventional if less lively.

There had been, to be sure, other magazines for children.

Besides *The Juvenile Miscellany*, early in the century, there were *Parley's Magazine, Merry's Museum, The Schoolmate* and a sprinkling of others, some of a Sunday-school nature; there was the indispensable *Youth's Companion*. But *Our Young Folks* was cut to a different pattern. Its publication marked the beginning of a new era in writing for boys and girls, when reading for recreation was accepted as right and desirable without the ulterior motive of satisfying a thirst for information.

Never was a magazine more auspiciously started. Like *The Atlantic Monthly* it had the interest of the foremost writers of the time. To the editorial board of their new periodical Ticknor and Fields called three persons, all with established reputations in literary circles, John T. Trowbridge, Gail Hamilton and Lucy Larcom. They brought to it high ideals of the possibilities of a good magazine for boys and girls. "It should be made to distance all competitors in value as it does in patronage," said Miss Larcom, when its financial success had become assured.

Most famous among the contributors of the initial number of January, 1865, was Harriet Beecher Stowe, the best-known woman writer in the country, then at the height of her popularity. Her story of "Hum, the Son of Buz," was given place of honor. Throughout the years she continued to write articles for *Our Young Folks;* in fact, practically everything that Mrs. Stowe intended for boys and girls was published originally in this magazine. *Little Pussy*

Willow, later brought out as a book, was one of the first of the country heroines to show a languid city miss the pleasures of healthful living. Theodore Roosevelt has recorded in his *Autobiography* how much he admired this demure and sensible heroine when he met her in the pages of *Our Young Folks*. Two serial stories from the hands of favorite writers for boys were continued through the twelve issues of 1865, one by Mayne Reid, *Afloat in the Forest*, typical adventure tale of that prolific writer; the other *Winning His Way*, signed "Carleton," pen name of Charles Carleton Coffin, noted war correspondent of the North. There were a story by Louisa Alcott, poems written by Lowell and Longfellow, and over the initials, "C. T.," Celia Thaxter's exquisite "Sandpiper" was given to the world.

Of the three editors it was probably John T. Trowbridge who contributed most largely to the pages of *Our Young Folks* as long as it lived, writing at times under assumed names as well as his own. Born in a log house in a clearing in the forest which then covered Genesee County, New York, Trowbridge early showed a love of nature and an absorbing interest in literature. By the time he was thirteen he was writing verses while eagerly gathering up a knowledge of books of various kinds. These tastes later brought him in contact with men of letters in New York and led him finally to Boston where he became associated with the group of writers for *The Atlantic Monthly*, an association which continued until his death.

Before his appointment as editor of *Our Young Folks*, Mr. Trowbridge had written several successful novels, *Neighbor Jackwood*, *Cudjo's Cave* and *The Three Scouts*, all colored by the problems of slavery and war. When he began to write for boys, he brought to the undertaking the practiced hand of an experienced author and a name familiar to readers of the best magazines of the day. *Our Young Folks* was secure of a feature of unquestioned popularity when *Jack Hazard and His Fortunes* appeared as a leading serial. From the memory of his own early life on the banks of the Erie Canal, Trowbridge drew the background for this story of real boy character. The gaunt horses, the muddy towpath, the clumsy scow were all familiar sights to him and he made them vivid to his readers. Jack Hazard, "the ragged little driver with a whip in one hand and a piece of bread-and-molasses in the other," calls forth our sympathy as he makes his escape with his one friend, the dog Lion, from his brutal father and the rough occupants of the canal boat. Countless boys have followed Jack's fortunes through the five books which comprise the Jack Hazard series. Besides these Mr. Trowbridge produced other books, some of which were first published in *St. Nicholas*.

Lucy Larcom invested the editorial board with good taste, genuine sympathy with childhood, and a strong moral sentiment which frequently expressed itself in her articles and poems. In *A New England Girlhood*, she wrote an enduring autobiography, introducing a remarkable group of young women who lived in the days when industrial problems were less complicated than they are now. Almost every month *Our Young Folks* contained a ballad or poem or prose sketch by this gentle lady, the friend of Whittier, collaborator with him in his two anthologies, *Child Life in Poetry* and *Child Life in Prose*. Through these admirable collections in their plain green covers many children have owed their introduction to "The Ugly Duckling" and "The Story Without an End," to "The Owl and the Pussy-Cat" and many an other poem and story whose inclusion showed Miss Larcom's genuine talent for selection. She was never quite happy signing her own name and preferred using initials, for while alliteration in pen names was the fashion of the day she did not care for it. The name of Lucy Larcom, its bearer felt, seemed like the adopted signatures of some of her contemporaries, "Minnie Myrtle," "Fanny Forrester" and "Grace Greenwood."

Gail Hamilton, the editor whose name appears in the second place on the early covers of *Our Young Folks*, was a member of the anti-slavery party in whose interests she wielded a sharp and vigorous pen. Her essays and papers for the general reader were accounted witty and she had a considerable circle of admirers, but her gifts to literature for children had no real importance. Mary Abigail Dodge, of Hamilton, Massachusetts, was the designation from which her pseudonym was derived. Disagreements with her publishers, Ticknor and Fields, brought about a severance of the relationship after a few years and her name was dropped from the cover, leaving Mr. Trowbridge and Miss Larcom to carry on alone.

Our Young Folks was less than a year old when its publishers developed their plan for still a third magazine and invited to their pleasant editorial rooms overlooking Boston Common a young man from New York who used to say in after life: "Though I am not genuine Boston, I am Boston-plated." Thomas Bailey Aldrich then became editor of *Every Saturday*, an eclectic weekly which drew largely from foreign periodicals. In October, 1868, "Marjorie's Almanac," a graceful little poem with real child interest, marked Mr. Aldrich's first appearance in *Our Young Folks*. The next year the inimitable *Story of a Bad Boy* was carried as a serial.

The Story of a Bad Boy stands as a landmark among American books for boys and girls. We count it as one of our unquestioned classics and venture to say that it will outlast everything else that Aldrich wrote. For felicity of style and clear-sighted interpretation of boy life it is unsurpassed. Written mainly at Portsmouth, the Rivermouth of Tom Bailey's boyhood, it was finished in a house on Pinckney Street, in Boston, passing naturally from there to the office of *Our Young Folks*. If it is idealized autobiography it yet possesses a universal appeal. Even the inevitable changes worked by time on the pastimes and manners of each new generation do not take away the reality of certain unforgettable incidents of the story. Every boy can enter with sympathy into Tom's sensations on that memorable Fourth of July when, his friends having scattered, Tom Bailey was faced with the empty glasses for twelve sixpenny ice creams, "strawberry and verneller mixed." And combined with all the humor and fun in which the book abounds, there is still that touch of sadness said to be inseparable from perfect art, as on the memorable pages which tell about little Binny Wallace drifting out to sea.

It must have been a particularly gratifying moment for the editors of this magazine for young people when they were able to announce the name of Charles Dickens among their authors. *Holiday Romance*, best known to us now by the story called "The Magic Fishbone," was issued in four installments in 1868, just after the novelist's American visit. In book form and with Bedford's delicious illustrations, the engaging tale of the Princess Alicia, her impecunious papa and her fairy godmother, still continues to tickle the fancy of humor-loving American children. In the same volume, too, Lucretia P. Hale introduced the Peterkin family to an appreciative audience of old and young, and William Henry's letters to his grandmother were produced, a packet at a time, from the desk of Mrs. Diaz. Between the orange covers there was plenty of laughter that year. Who can wonder that Theodore Roosevelt, looking back at those halcyon days, declared that there never was such a magazine? With the names of Whittier and Lowell and Longfellow, with Bayard Taylor's chapters on the *Boys of Other*

Countries, Mrs. Whitney's *We Girls*, Dr. Isaac Hayes's *Cast Away in the Cold*, and many other notable numbers to be found in the index, such a claim has its merits.

All that a good modern magazine can offer had been included. For their day the illustrations were worthy of the text, representative work of such artists as Winslow Homer, John Gilbert and H. L. Stephens. Special departments for correspondence and puzzles had a place, but in one respect a great and significant difference between these old periodicals and those now published may be noticed—advertisements are entirely absent from their pages. It was a time when magazines could live for a while on their subscription lists alone.

Nine years seems a short life for a publication so successful and so well loved. When the time came, as it did in 1874, for *Our Young Folks* to take leave of its first home, it was not from any failure in popularity or prestige, it was only one more example of the insecurity of business undertakings. So the fine young monthly was sold to Scribner's in New York, and became the foundation of its still more famous successor, *St. Nicholas*, under the direction of Mary Mapes Dodge, a truly great editor.

GOOD OLD "ST. NICHOLAS"
AND ITS CONTEMPORARIES

XI

STANDING side by side in a row on the shelves of fortunate children's libraries is a line of large red books, stamped generously in black and gold. Perhaps they may be considered too precious for careless handling, but the knowing child who likes to make discoveries in books has already claimed them as a treasure house of riches. They are the bound volumes of the monthly magazine, *St. Nicholas*, in the days of its prime. Within these red covers lies the very kernel of American books for children, published during a period of more than thirty years.

Now and then, when readers who were young in the nineties get together, you may hear them talk of the glorious days when *St. Nicholas* flourished, bringing out, month by month, all their favorite stories. And some there are whose memories go still further back, who can remember what it was like to wait impatiently for the latest chapter of "Donald and Dorothy," or the whimsical travels of "Davy and the Goblin." They speak of it with affection. "There never was a magazine like it," they say.

So, too, thought the readers of *Our Young Folks*, or *The Riverside Magazine*, about the periodical they had learned to love. But *St. Nicholas* was, indeed, different. There is a lighthearted quality, a gaiety in its appearance which could not have been achieved in the earlier magazines. Children who never knew it in the days of its publication find its bound volumes as satisfying reading as newer books, as modern in the spirit of its contents. Behind the making of such a magazine there had to be a creative personality. To think of the great days of *St. Nicholas* is to think of Mary Mapes Dodge, its first editor.

From a girlhood home presided over by a father who combined scholarship and a scientist's inquiring mind with the gift of storyteller, she drew a spacious background of association with books and people. There were always guests in that home, guests representing New York's circle of literary men and illustrious artists, whose talk threw off sparks to kindle the thoughts and ambitions of an eager girl. Her warm and buoyant nature which surrounded her with friends gave her, too, a deep respect for children and an understanding of their interests. This was further strengthened by her close companionship with her two young sons. It was for them she had written *Hans Brinker* in 1865.

Mary Mapes Dodge was already conducting a successful juvenile department in *Hearth and Home*, a New York weekly edited by Edward Eggleston, when she was asked to undertake the editorship of a magazine devoted entirely to children. It was projected by the owners of *Scribner's Monthly*, then in its third year, and destined to become later the *Century Magazine*.

The early seventies was an arid time for children's books, no less than for literature in general, save for the small group of New England writers. Parents were worried, too, over the prevalence of "dime novels," but a sufficient body of suitable literature for children was not yet in sight. It took vision to see a future for a new magazine which should aim to please children rather than their elders, a bright and gay magazine, with many pictures by the foremost artists. Roswell Smith had that vision. Mrs. Dodge once said that the success of *St. Nicholas* rested in large measure upon the generosity of its founder. As one of the owners of *Scribner's Monthly*, he wanted to enlarge the company's influence, for he believed it was possible to make such a magazine more attractive than any hitherto published. On Mrs. Dodge's acceptance of the post of editor, its inception depended.

Scribner's Monthly, for July, 1873, contains an unsigned article on "Children's Magazines," expressing some fresh and constructive ideas, as pertinent now as they were seventy years ago. The article is significant because these views, held by Mary Mapes Dodge, show what lay behind her leadership for more than three decades in the production of a literature for children. "The children's magazine must not be a milk-and-water variety of the periodical for adults. In fact, it needs to be stronger, truer, bolder, more uncompromising than the other," she said. The publisher's announcements echoed these words. There must be entertainment, no less than information; the spirit of laughter would be evoked; there would be "no sermonizing, no wearisome spinning out of facts, no rattling of the dry bones of history," while all priggishness was condemned.

Heralded by such sane and inviting pledges, the first issue of *St. Nicholas* appeared in November, 1873, opening with a letter from the editor, giving the reasons that lay behind the choice of the name for the new magazine. That happy inspiration linked *St. Nicholas* forever with New York and its patron saint.

Assisting Mrs. Dodge was Frank Stockton, who had previously worked with her on *Hearth and Home*. He was to serve as Associate Editor of *St. Nicholas* for seven years. During those years, and afterward, his short stories were a notable feature, gladdening the pages of *St. Nicholas* for many issues with their inimitable turns of fancy, delicious sense of humor and gentle philosophy, always kindly, but never dull. They were phrased, too, in a charming style. John T. Trowbridge joined the staff in the first year, though with a heavy heart, since his own well-loved paper had been sold by its Boston owners and merged in the new magazine.

He did not know, when he planned his last number of *Our Young Folks*, that this was to happen, and his card in an early *St. Nicholas* has a natural note of sadness. "That I do not mourn the loss of our little favorite, I will not pretend," he said. "It filled its place and it is gone; and we believe from its grave violets will spring to blossom amid the leaves of a more beautiful and beloved successor." His connection with *St. Nicholas* lasted until 1916. Officially, Horace E. Scudder had no place in the *St. Nicholas* organization, yet as a congenial and trusted authority he was often consulted by the editor. Not only were his experiences in editing the short-lived *Riverside Magazine* of value to her, but the two friends were in complete agreement on the essentials of children's literature, a field where their joint influence was profound.

Mrs. Dodge wanted the new periodical to be a beautiful production and a playground as well. She brought to her post not only unusual literary discrimination but a joyous spirit, radiating enthusiasm and energy, calling out the best and most sincere writing from her authors, making them eager to win her approval, often tempting them into new fields. Her own contributions were more numerous than anyone guessed. While the initials, M. M. D., were a familiar sight at the foot of verses and articles, she also masqueraded each month as Jack-in-the-Pulpit and The Little Schoolma'am, through whose voices she could express editorial opinions and give sensible advice. Occasionally, at other times, she hid her identity in the name of Joel Stacy.

The seventies were made memorable by the work of many well-known personages. Poems by Bryant and Whittier, Celia Thaxter and Lucy Larcom indicate the interest taken by writers of established reputation. Month by month, Louisa Alcott's *Eight Cousins* and *Under the Lilacs* invited constant readers. The popular serials by Trowbridge, *Fast Friends* and *The Young Surveyor*, and Noah Brooks' *The Boy Emigrants* captured the boys who perceived the authenticity of backgrounds based on personal adventure. T. B. Aldrich, Lucretia P. Hale, Sarah Orne Jewett, Susan Coolidge and Laura E. Richards were frequent contributors during the decade. Articles on astronomy by R. A. Proctor and on bird life by Olive Thorne Miller fostered scientific tastes, not then nourished by school programs. Howard Pyle's name first appears as author–illustrator of a fairy tale in November, 1877. Later his fine books, *Otto of the Silver Hand* and *The Story of King Arthur*, came out as installments in *St. Nicholas* with his own distinguished pictures.

The eighties carried on many of the same authors, adding for boy adventure long stories by W. O. Stoddard. Mrs. Dodge's *Donald and Dorothy*, Frances Courtenay Baylor's *Juan and Juanita*, Harris' *Daddy Jake the Runaway* and Baldwin's *Northern Myths*, all belong to that period. It was in 1885–1886 that *Little Lord Fauntleroy*, most famous of all *St. Nicholas* children, took the country by storm. Frances Hodgson Burnett did not consider herself a writer for children, but she was willing to try her hand at the request of Mary Mapes

Dodge. With the appearance of *Little Lord Fauntleroy*, a great surprise was in store for editor and author alike. Pictured by Reginald Birch, the courtly little hero, with his velvet suit, lace collar and forgiving spirit, became unbelievably famous. Though never a favorite with boys, his story was translated into several other languages, and after he took the stage in the person of nine-year-old Elsie Leslie, he won the hearts of countless theater audiences.

The high point of *St. Nicholas* in the nineties was John Bennett's classic story of the reign of Queen Elizabeth, careful in historical detail and full of action, about the strolling players and the boy with the golden voice, *Master Skylark*. *Lady Jane* was another serial greatly enjoyed during those years. It was a New Orleans story, by Mrs. C. V. Jamison, one of the first of the mystery tales and felt by girls to be very exciting.

Pleasure in the *St. Nicholas* contents was greatly enhanced by the wealth of pictures from the hands of distinguished illustrators of the day, or, infrequently, by reproductions from famous paintings. "The pictures must have the greatest variety consistent with simplicity, beauty and unity. They should be heartily conceived and well executed, and they must be suggestive, attractive, and epigrammatic." The choice was varied enough to include such diverse examples as Delaroche's touching "Children of Edward IV in the Tower" and Arthur Rackham's ivory-toned drawings for Mother Goose. The names of F. S. Church, George Wharton Edwards and Joseph Pennell may all be found in files of *St. Nicholas*. For fun, there were E. B. Bensell's spirited illustrations for Frank Stockton's stories, J. G. Francis' *Cheerful Cats*, and the forerunner of the Brownies from the hand of Palmer Cox. They are held as fondly in memory as the stories.

Through articles in the volumes of *St. Nicholas* can be traced the changing American scene of the late nineteenth century, the effect of inventions and industrial development, the shifting of emphasis in social life. We can follow the rising tide of the school story, seen first in 1882 with Eggleston's *The Hoosier School-boy;* eight years later with the introduction of athletics in Allen French's *Junior Cup;* reaching its full-fledged state by emphasizing sport, in Barbour's *Crimson Sweater*, in 1906. Dan Beard's widely popular papers on handicraft and camping were abreast of the times in the eighties; equally modern in 1906 was Tudor Jenks' account of flying machines, advanced by 1910 to an article on "Boys and the Air-Ship" by Francis Arnold Collins.

The Departments claimed full measure of attention from children of different tastes. For young children, the early numbers carried a simple story in large type which could be easily read by beginners. The Letter Box brought correspondents to children in country homes, the Bird-Defenders encouraged humanitarian efforts, the Agassiz Association stimulated observation in the field of science long before the public school curriculums included more than physiology.

In 1899, St. Nicholas League, directed for ten years by Albert Bigelow Paine, began its promotion of the arts by distribution of medals and honorable mention, and by printing original work of a sufficiently meritorious standard.

In its happy days *St. Nicholas* went everywhere. Its subscribers were scattered through cities and towns, on distant ranches and isolated farms from one end of the American continent to the other. English-reading children in many other lands welcomed it. Young Rudyard Kipling used to read it and, years after, wrote some of the Jungle Book stories for its pages because of the pleasure given Mrs. Dodge by one of his Indian animal tales. A story in the bound volume of *St. Nicholas* for 1884, picked up in the Oakland Public Library, so gripped Jack London, a boy of sixteen, that he determined to give up his life as a tough young "water rat" and offer his services to the state fish patrol. He made good in that service and was proud to have his story, "The Cruise of the Dazzler," published in the magazine in 1902.

Edna St. Vincent Millay, as a girl in Rockland, Maine, read *St. Nicholas* and joined the League, in whose columns her early poems appeared repeatedly, with honorable mention. About the same time, too, *St. Nicholas* went to a lonely farmhouse in New Hampshire, bringing heartening approval of the boyish drawings of young Robert E. Jones, whose talents have burgeoned forth in stage design.

After the death of Mary Mapes Dodge in 1905, the task of editing *St. Nicholas* was assumed by William Fayal Clarke, who had worked with her from its beginning. Mr. Clarke continued as editor until 1927. It seems to be a hard fact, recognized in the publishing world, that a magazine for children is seldom, if ever, self-sustaining. In 1930, the Century Company sold *St. Nicholas* away from New York, but the decline of the old magazine could not be arrested, and its last days are best forgotten.

St. Nicholas was only five years old when another renowned New York publishing house decided to add to its monthly and weekly periodicals for adults one designed especially for children. Nor could it have been surprising at the time that Harper and Brothers took such a step, for of all the American publishers this was the one with a lengthy roll of authors who had for years given particular attention to writing for children.

A prospectus circulated in the fall of 1879 announces: "We shall begin next month the publication of an illustrated journal of amusement and instruction, to be called *Harper's Young People*." For twenty years, this lively magazine held an important place in the hearts of American boys and girls, rivaling *St. Nicholas* in the opinion of some readers. Although it was a weekly the subscription price was only a dollar and a half a year, and the standard of writing was high. The aim of the sponsors was to "stimulate and satisfy the intelligent curiosity of boys and girls," by the inclusion of factual articles on nature, art and travel, with stories to gratify the imagination and with plenty of fun.

Placed side by side with the first issue of *St. Nicholas* the new magazine suffers by comparison as the print is fine and the format cheap. Later, these faults were corrected, the size of the paper was doubled and eventually the name changed to *Harper's Round Table*.

Kirk Munroe was the first editor of *Harper's Young People*, serving in that capacity for three years and writing for the magazine as long as it lasted. He had roved far over the United States, had been a surveyor in the West, knew Custer and Buffalo Bill. *The Flamingo Feather*, one of the best of his Indian stories, concerned the Seminoles of Florida. *Derrick Sterling* was about a boy in the mines, one of the earliest children's books about an industry. Munroe's stories were immensely popular, but as they were often carelessly written they have not survived.

Another favorite and prolific writer whose serials often appeared in *Harper's Young People* was James Otis (Kaler). Only one of his books merits recalling. *Toby Tyler*, foremost for decades among stories about the circus, has qualities that have kept it alive, appearing from time to time with new pictures, for over sixty years. Toby Tyler, who had run away from home allured by the glittering splendor of a traveling circus, was realistically drawn. In the ten uncomfortable weeks the boy spent with the big top his dearest friend was Mr. Stubbs with his little brown hands and expressive face, the compassionate clutch of his paw, the wise look in his grave eyes. Countless children have been able to believe with Toby that the aged monkey knew what was said to him and might even talk if he tried. Over Mr. Stubbs' moving fate genuine tears have been shed, yet the story never lapses into sentimentality.

Many of the *St. Nicholas* authors wrote also for *Harper's Young People* and many of the same illustrators were to be found working for both magazines. Howard Pyle turned to *Harper's Young People* when he found his first outlet overstocked with his fables. *The Merry Adventures of Robin Hood* was published there, but the few pictures then used were not included in the finished volume. As *Harper's Young People* gained in good looks, approval of it as a "noble storehouse of good reading" grew apace and, like *St. Nicholas*, it had its English edition.

The third periodical for boys and girls, flourishing in the 1880's, was *Wide Awake*, published in Boston by the Lothrop Company. Keyed for the same public as the other two magazines, it had its devoted followers throughout the course of its life (1875-1893). *Wide Awake* was designed somewhat in the likeness of *St. Nicholas*, similar in size with many pictures, and pages in large print for the youngest readers. Early volumes drew occasionally from English sources and George Macdonald's lovely *Double Story* was serialized the first year.

All three of these periodicals were analyzed in *Reading for the Young*, that fine list of books and magazine articles begun by John F. Sargent in 1886 and continued by his sisters.

Probably the most warmly cherished books growing out of *Wide Awake* are Margaret Sidney's Pepper books, beginning with *Five Little Peppers and How They Grew*. Unfortunately the series was continued too long and suffered after the first three volumes from declining vigor. The Peppers were a large and happy family abounding with high spirits and hearty activity, but with small material assets, so they were obliged to manage carefully and "make things do." Their problems are not unlike those of the March family of an earlier generation.

THE GOLDEN AGE

XII

ECHOES from the Didactic Era were passing away when *Books for the Young* was published in 1882. Caroline Hewins' reading list says almost as much by its omissions as by its inclusions. No Peter Parleys are to be found in it, no Sunday-school stories, sentimentality has disappeared.

The decade of the 1880's, preceded by the quickening effect of the Centennial four years earlier, was a brilliant period in American children's literature. Seeds planted by the great editors were coming to fullness in this period, burgeoning into a more mature and just appraisal of the "juvenile" as an honorable contribution to literature which could no longer be ignored. The children's field shared in the changes affecting books in general—the greater consciousness of national life, the trend toward more realistic fiction. At the same time there was a flowing tide of imaginative power.

Realistic fiction continued to thrive under the hands of the

New England group of women writers, whose healthy tales of normal home life had begun in the seventies, or earlier. Louisa Alcott's *Under the Lilacs* and *Jack and Jill*, though written within the shadow of her mother's death and that of "Amy," showed little of the sadness their author was hiding. Susan Coolidge (Sarah Chauncey Woolsey), an adopted New Englander, added to her honest, unaffected *Katy* books; Mary P. Wells Smith pictured the freedom of farm life in the *Jolly Good Times* stories. To satisfy boys' tastes Trowbridge, Brooks and Stoddard still carried on. But for the surge of fine books of the imagination, with one exception, we must look beyond the borders of New England.

Where the three books by Thomas Bulfinch had long stood alone with Hawthorne's Greek fairy tales to introduce boys and girls to classic myths, James Baldwin, an educator from the Wabash country, and Sidney Lanier, a poet of the South, now retold the heroic legends for young people in books that have become classics.

There were few books in the Friends Community when James Baldwin was growing up in Indiana, a backwoods boy who thought the log cabin in which he was born was the center of the world. Yet the pleasantest memories of his early years were associated with his tiny library, and his first and lasting ambition was to write books himself. When the time came to do so in earnest, he did not turn to the scenes of his boyhood for inspiration, as did Edward Eggleston who was writing at the same time, describing with fidelity and humor the rough manners of a small country neighborhood in *The Hoosier School-boy*. Instead, Baldwin recalled his own tastes when he hungered for reading and so wrote of a dragon slayer and a splendid hero.

The Story of Siegfried and *The Story of Roland* have not been superseded by later versions of these old tales. For the *Siegfried*, Baldwin drew from the Eddas and the Nibelungenlied, changing and recasting these and other renderings of the ancient myths so as to embody the inherent qualities of poetic literature in the childhood of the world. For the *Roland*, he blended fact and fiction as they were set down by "song writers and poets of five centuries and as many languages." Through both books blow the winds of adventure, daring and loyalties to spread the fires of youthful aspiration.

Sidney Lanier, in *The Boy's King Arthur*, followed closely the history of the brave world of romance as it was set forth by Sir Thomas Malory. When Lanier felt that the old chronicler's words were too archaic to be easily understood, he added a modern equivalent in brackets, but he did this sparingly so that the style is not injured. Interest in the lofty ideals of knighthood had been nourished in the poet's southern boyhood, when deeds of valor and chivalry kindled his own imagination. Over the years *The Boy's King Arthur* has passed along these high ideals to the young manhood of many ardent boys.

In the very center of the Golden Age stands the name of Howard Pyle. Four matchless books of his creating belong in the harvest of the 1880's, two more in the nineties, followed within fifteen years by the four great volumes of the Arthurian cycle. And in each of these books there was the perfect harmony between written words and pictures which comes only as the rare gift of twofold talent.

"My ambition in days gone by," wrote Howard Pyle, "was to write a really notable adult book, but now I am glad that I have made literary friends of the children rather than older folk. In one's mature years one forgets the books that one reads, but the stories of childhood leave an indelible impression, and their author always has a niche in the temple of memory from which the image is never cast out to be thrown into the rubbish heap of things that are outgrown and outlived."

Best loved, and judged the most perfect of Pyle's work, is the *Robin Hood*, still fresh in its appeal, still merry and unspoiled, still full of the outdoor world which urgently calls young hearts to the greenwood. It was the book longest growing in the heart of Howard Pyle. He had been writing animal fables for *St. Nicholas* for several years, as a young man's first literary ventures in New York, but, insistently, his mind turned back to the old English ballads which his mother had read to him in his Delaware boyhood. He had loved Percy's *Reliques of Ancient English Poetry* then; he felt the stories would be loved by other boys and girls.

The time was ripe in 1883 for *The Merry Adventures of*

Robin Hood. Sidney Lanier and James Baldwin had introduced heroes from legend and romance whose deeds, touched with the miraculous, were on an exalted scale; they were knights of the first rank in the kingdom, always in deadly earnest. In contrast, Robin Hood was neither noble nor an aristocrat, and the handful of ballads recounting his deeds have been retold in lighthearted mirth. All is blithe in England —

> "at the dawn of day in the merry May-time when hedgerows are green and flowers bedeck the meadows; daisies pied and yellow cuckoo buds and fair primroses all along the briery hedges; when apple buds blossom and sweet birds sing, the lark at dawn of day, the throstle cock and cuckoo; when lads and lassies look upon each other with sweet thoughts; when busy housewives spread their linen to bleach upon the green grass."

In word pictures such as these, the stage was set for the tales of the Great Fair at Nottingham, for Robin's bout with the tall stranger, for Little John's feats at the shooting match, for the shouts of laughter over the mishaps of the luckless Sheriff of Nottingham, for the entrance of the "proudest of the Plantagenets." Scudder's *Children's Book* had contained several of the Robin Hood ballads. Now, through successive numbers of *Harper's Young People*, fortunate children were meeting the outlaw band, clothed in Lincoln green, in the Forest of Sherwood or in the fields of barley and corn in

Nottinghamshire. When the book with its superb illustrations was published it met with applause that has grown rather than diminished with the years, inspiring the tribute of a third generation who count this book first favorite in their libraries.

Robin Hood was a young man's book, written when Howard Pyle was thirty years old. From his pleasure in writing it and from his readers' pleasure, the author discovered his ability to write acceptably for children and went on to elaborate themes from the old fairy tales in *Pepper and Salt* and *The Wonder Clock*, first published in *Harper's Young People*. Adorned with drawings and decorations, these two books have a vitality that constantly wakens a response from the children and satisfies their sense of fun. The beauty of line in the pictures has been all but lost in recent printings from worn plates.

Master of the short story at a time when this form of fiction was the fashion, Frank Stockton discovered early that writing meant more to him than the art of engraving for which he had been trained. Starting with *The Riverside Magazine* and continuing in *St. Nicholas*, this vivacious, ingenious man drew upon his inexhaustible imagination to produce one amusing story after another, combining the most incongruous happenings with a fine literary touch, distinctly the writer's own. Fun and philosophy are so cunningly united in them that, while Stockton's stories are ostensibly for children, they have a nearly comparable attraction for those who are older. Never localized, anything might come to pass in the world of Frank Stockton. His stories came from a sunny nature with a wit that left no barb or sting.

All sorts of odd characters people these fanciful tales. Besides the Floating Prince, there is the naïve old Bee-man who kept a beehive in his pocket so that he could be sure of having something to eat wherever he went; there is the Queen who was a collector of buttonholes and had an unpopular Museum; there is the Jolly-cum-pop who liked hunting; there is the Reformed Pirate, knitting so quietly in his rocking chair, and there are countless others who deserve to be remembered. They are just as pleasant to read about now as they were in the 1880's.

While Stockton had been turning out his lighthearted fairy tales for nearly two decades before *Davy and the Goblin* delighted *St. Nicholas* readers (1885), its author Charles Carryl derived in no way from the older American. Rather, the inspiration of this Boston father who told his own children about Davy's adventures came from Lewis Carroll, of Oxford, England. What happened on a stormy Christmas Eve, after eight-year-old Davy had been reading *Alice in Wonderland*, has touches suggesting that Davy's Believing Voyage could scarcely have been undertaken except for someone's acquaintance with scenes down the rabbit hole or in the Looking Glass country. This is frankly admitted on the first page.

Far from being an imitation, however, *Davy and the Gob-lin* is a kind of companion piece which proves specially attractive to little boys. They accept confidingly Davy's encounters with the Cockalorum, the Butterscotchmen, the Forty Thieves, Sindbad and Robinson Crusoe when he travels with the Goblin, riding through the air over strange lands on the big Dutch clock with sponge cakes as cushions. If Lewis Carroll's wisdom and philosophy are lacking, still there is good nonsense sprinkled with mouth-filling words and such capital verse as the chronicles of the Walloping Window-Blind and the Piccadilly Daisy which fall trippingly from the tongue.

From Charles Carryl came also *The Admiral's Caravan*, published in *St. Nicholas* in 1892.

Three more important characters appeared in children's literature early in the 1880's, Brer Rabbit, Brer Fox and Uncle Remus. Is there anyone who can forget the story of "The Wonderful Tar-Baby," with Brer Rabbit "pacin' down de road—lipperty-clipperty, clipperty-lipperty—dez ez sassy ez a jay bird," while Brer Fox, "he lay low"?

Georgia had already made entrance into the widening arena of children's books with Lanier's *Boy's King Arthur;* this was a lighter note. South and North received it with undisguised enjoyment. Lovable old Uncle Remus was a type fast disappearing, but in those who had been young in the South he revived intimate childhood memories of old folks from whom girls and boys had heard just such animal stories as those told by Uncle Remus. They saw themselves reflected in "Miss Sally's little boy," without a name. Northern children, who had never known such a relationship, made fascinating discoveries about plantation life and reveled in the humor of the tales.

Here was a cast of animals who talked and acted like real people. Yet they were not like the Toad and the Mole in "Thumbelina," not quite like Alice's Rabbit, not at all like Aesop's Beasts who were never content unless pointing a Moral. Together with personality, here were present mischievousness, a shrewd philosophy, a dramatic triumph of helplessness, a kinship between animals and humans.

Joel Chandler Harris turned for his sources to the familiar folk tales of the Southern Negro and he created in Uncle Remus the memorable portrait of a born storyteller with a faithfulness that could hardly have been achieved at a later period. Simple and serious, patient and devoted, sympathetic with children because he was himself childlike, sharing with his listeners a vivid concern in the animals' doings, he was quick to draw comparisons between animals and "fokes," and he was constantly mindful of the little boy's duty toward his family traditions.

The young Georgia editor was surprised by the acclaim which met *Uncle Remus: His Songs and His Sayings*, when it was given book form in 1880. He was even amused when learned journals discussed it as an important contribution to folklore. Folklore the stories are, as Harris knew perfectly well, but he had not printed these tales for their scholarly value and had chosen only those best suited for entertainment through the art of a natural storyteller. Much has been written about the Uncle Remus stories, their humor, their African origin, their expression of the imagination of a race which chose the most harmless of animals to be victor by its wits. Mr. Harris was only glad that he had made children happy. Fifteen years after its first appearance *Uncle Remus: His Songs and His Sayings* was reissued with the inimitable and perfect pictures by A. B. Frost who brought fresh vitality to Brer Rabbit, Brer Fox and the other animals. All attempts to retell the tales without the authentic dialect have been a failure.

Out of the South a few years later came another book in which an old Negro has a place. The Virginia gentleman, who called back memories of his boyhood to write a wartime story untouched by bitterness, had a background unlike that of Joel Chandler Harris, but his Old Balla was as true a part of the household as Uncle Remus was of Miss Sally's.

Thomas Nelson Page was writing romantic stories for adults when the idea of *Two Little Confederates* formed in his mind. He wanted to bring about a better understanding between North and South and his generous book does just that. Full of the charm of a vanished time, this home life story rests upon actual conditions surrounding his own Virginia home during the Civil War. The opening chapter of *Two Little Confederates* describes Oakland where Willy and Frank lived:

> "It was not a handsome place as modern ideas go, but down in Old Virginia where the standard was different from the later one, it passed in old times as one of the best places in all that region."

The future Ambassador to Italy was eight years old and his brother younger when the war began. Their father had earnestly hoped for peace but like so many others went with his state when it seceded. Troops from both sides passed through and around Oakland and the two boys saw soldiers often in the four years before Appomattox. They came to experience acutely the hardships and griefs of invasion, for the story is practically autobiographic and Mr. Page had good reason to know what Willy did and how he felt. Abundant humor is to be found in *Two Little Confederates*, sadness, suspense and the salt of charity and common humanity in its good writing. As the first book to give American children living far from the scenes of battle an idea of what it might mean to be in the path of war, it was a revelation, yet the temper is very different from the partisan stories of the Revolutionary War.

Aside from stories about Indians, not always trustworthy, American authors for young people had seldom tried their hand at writing historical fiction. In *Books for the Young* the names of British writers in this class, Sir Walter Scott,

Charlotte M. Yonge and George A. Henty, are more conspicuous than those of any American except Cooper. But that very year *The Prince and the Pauper* had appeared, and Miss Hewins was quick to include the title in her reading list.

Whatever librarians and mothers of that time thought about placing *Tom Sawyer* in the hands of children, they never doubted that Mark Twain had written a real children's book which might wholeheartedly be accepted for boys. *The Prince and the Pauper* with its plot of the exchange of places between Tom Canty and the Boy King Edward VI brought into the open for children the gulf between the palaces of royalty and the dwellings of the poor in the days of the Tudors — not a very likely plot perhaps, but one into which boys and girls could enter with sympathy. Mark Twain, the democrat, with his hatred of shams and false values, had thrown a bright light on injustices and inequalities little perceived by American children in their restricted study of history at school.

And again, it was Howard Pyle whose literary skill and feeling for the past strengthened children's literature by another distinguished book. He had been steeping himself, ever since his *Robin Hood*, in medieval manners and deeds, and *Otto of the Silver Hand* was the result. It brought the Middle Ages to life for boys and girls, not only of the eighties and nineties, but of years to come. Otto's affecting story, with its shadow of tragedy, embraces the days of the robber barons in Germany.

Here are all the trappings of a feudal stronghold in the dark and ancient castle of Drachenfels, with its drawbridge and portcullis, its men of arms and weapons of war. Here at the White Cross on the Hill is displayed a no less true aspect of the age in the sunny old monastery gardens. In both places, against harsh and cruel customs or self-denying charity, we see the slender form of little Otto whose endurance and noble spirit are brought into bold relief by the creative imagination of Howard Pyle. A few more years brought Myles Falworth as vitally to the fore in *Men of Iron*, one of the best medieval tales we have. These two, with John Bennett's *Master Skylark*, make a rewarding heritage of historical fiction from the nineteenth century.

Secure of a permanent place in English literature, Mark Twain's third book about a boy is claimed by every age. To bar *Adventures of Huckleberry Finn* from a list of children's classics now is as unthinkable as it would have been to include it in the year of its publication (1885). In all the range of our fiction, said Joel Chandler Harris, "there is no more wholesome book than *Huckleberry Finn*. It is history, it is romance, it is life. Here we behold human characters stripped of all tiresome details; we see people growing and living; we laugh at their humor, share their griefs and in the midst of it all, behold, we are taught the lesson of honesty, justice and mercy."

Little Lord Fauntleroy ran in *St. Nicholas* as a serial in 1885, and its progress in popularity was swift and overwhelming.

Mrs. Burnett idealized in it her own relationship with one of her boys, and it pleased more parents than did *Huckleberry Finn*. Frances Hodgson Burnett was nothing if not romantic. She did not care so much about realism, she wished that fairies would "come in fashion again," and she liked to be considered a fairy herself. Her *Sara Crewe* is the veritable Cinderella type of story that children love. One short significant conversation in this book, when Sara is helping Ermengarde, a dull schoolmate, with her history lesson, illustrates entertainingly Mrs. Burnett's feeling for the part imagination plays in the lives of certain children.

> " 'It sounds nicer than it seems in the book' [Ermengarde] would say. 'I never cared about Mary Queen of Scots, before, and I always hated the French Revolution, but you make it seem like a story.' 'It is a story,' Sara would answer. 'They are all stories. Everything is a story—everything in this world. You are a story—I am a story—Miss Minchin is a story. You can make a story out of anything.' 'I can't,' said Ermengarde."

It was inevitable that Laura Richards should write books. Everything about her bringing up, her associations in childhood and early youth, all pointed that way. Besides, she had children of her own to listen to and applaud her inventions. Her nonsense verses inspired by Edward Lear whose limericks she had always known began early in the magazines, long before Lear had died, an old man; but her first complete book, *Five Mice in a Mouse-trap*, came out in 1880. Now, with these stories for the youngest, she was fairly launched on a lifetime of employing her abilities as children's author.

Other books of easy reading followed. *Four Feet, Two Feet, and No Feet* she wrote only in part, editing the rest to help little children explore the animal world. Then, in the same decade she started the Hildegarde books, and for the next fifteen years Mrs. Richards devoted her time to writing for young girls. In after days she was often critical of these early volumes, wishing she could rewrite them. Yet, notwithstanding their obvious faults, the Hildegarde series gave pleasure to hundreds of girls, also inciting in them an ambition to read the books and poems that Hildegarde liked.

About this time, too, a pioneer kindergartner in California, Kate Smith, not yet Kate Douglas Wiggin, was composing two books to further a Cause. *The Birds' Christmas Carol* and *The Story of Patsy*, written in San Francisco and bound in paper, were both sold for the benefit of the Free Kindergartens and were not intended for publication. Little did the young teacher dream that her Christmas story would one day be translated into French, Swedish, German and Japanese; that scenes from it would be dramatized and become highly esteemed for amateur production. Christmas after Christmas, since the eighties, this appealing story has called forth a warmth of affection for friendly little Carol and ripples of laughter over the vision of the Ruggleses making preparation for their Dinner Party, in which we catch a foreshadowing of the creation of *Rebecca of Sunnybrook Farm*.

Looking back at the animated procession of American girls moving through the books of the last quarter of the nineteenth century, the figure of Betty Leicester stands out in the front rank. Sarah Orne Jewett, to whom we owe her, wrote no other full-length book for girls, but her short stories had been printed in young people's magazines constantly after their appearance in the *Riverside* and older girls had become acquainted with her exquisite cameos in published collections and in the pages of *The Atlantic Monthly*. Some of them knew the delicate touch with which the lovely story of Sylvia, in *A White Heron*, had been etched.

Betty Leicester begins and ends with a journey. Tideshead, where Betty Leicester visited with her great-aunts, becomes a real place before the summer is over. So do the new friends she made there and the old ones who grew dearer seem real under Miss Jewett's skillful hand. Without excitement, without the accessories of modern invention, she weaves interest and charm into the story of an uneventful summer when a fifteen-year-old girl learned to live with other people and to know herself.

The Golden Age was further characterized by interest in books about wild life and the outdoor world. *St. Nicholas* nourished this awakening through the Agassiz Association, and Olive Thorne Miller followed her *Little Folks in Feathers and Fur* with studies about bird life. Then, too, the flood of books on how to make and do things was inaugurated by Dan Beard in *The American Boys' Handybook*. All in all, it was a great period for children's books in America, vitalized by a force which overflowed into the nineties sorely in need of it, for by the turn of the century the flame was burning low.

There was to be a full quarter of a century of marking time, but in this Golden Age were the seeds of that new flowering of children's books which opened in 1920. The decade of the 1880's saw the awakening to the richness of folklore, felt the inspiration drawn from classic hero tales, experienced the leavening of humor and fantasy. The field was being prepared for the influences, dimly discerned by the far-sighted, of those invigorating currents of literature brought to bear by many people coming from other lands to America. But as the nineteenth century closed, it could not be known what great wealth of art and color and life the newcomers would bring to American children's books.